Return to the Eternal Abode

SUNY series in Islam
―――――――
Seyyed Hossein Nasr, editor

Return to the Eternal Abode
A Sufi Dialogue with Seyyed Hossein Nasr

AMIRA EL-ZEIN

Published by State University of New York Press, Albany

© 2025 State University of New York

All rights reserved

Printed in the United States of America

No part of this book may be used or reproduced in any manner whatsoever without written permission. No part of this book may be stored in a retrieval system or transmitted in any form or by any means including electronic, electrostatic, magnetic tape, mechanical, photocopying, recording, or otherwise without the prior permission in writing of the publisher.

Links to third-party websites are provided as a convenience and for informational purposes only. They do not constitute an endorsement or an approval of any of the products, services, or opinions of the organization, companies, or individuals. SUNY Press bears no responsibility for the accuracy, legality, or content of a URL, the external website, or for that of subsequent websites.

For information, contact State University of New York Press, Albany, NY
www.sunypress.edu

Library of Congress Cataloging-in-Publication Data

Names: El-Zein, Amira, author. | Nasr, Seyyed Hossein, author.
Title: Return to the eternal abode : Sufi dialogues with Seyyed Hossein Nasr / Amira El-Zein.
Description: Albany : State University of New York Press, [2025] | Series: SUNY series in Islam | Includes bibliographical references and index.
Identifiers: LCCN 2024027044 | ISBN 9798855800784 (hardcover : alk. paper) | ISBN 9798855800791 (ebook) | ISBN 9798855800777 (pbk. : alk. paper)
Subjects: LCSH: Sufism.
Classification: LCC BP189 .E49 2025 | DDC 297.4—dc23/eng/20240911
LC record available at https://lccn.loc.gov/2024027044

Contents

Introduction: Thirst for the Source	1
1. Sufism and Creativity	19
2. Sufism and Cosmology	49
3. Sufism and the Environment	93
4. Sufism and Poetry	131
5. Art and Sufism	165
6. Sufism and Modernity	193
Notes	209
Index	213

Introduction
Thirst for the Source

AMIRA EL-ZEIN

These conversations between Seyyed Hossein Nasr and myself took place in Washington, DC, over a long period of time. Now the time has finally come for them to see the light.

I decided to meet with Dr. Nasr after I had read most of his works. I was preoccupied at that time, as I am today, with the question of the environment, the degradation of nature, and the sacred origin of knowledge. As a poet, I was also interested in his interpretations of Sufi poetry, especially that of Rumi, who remains my favorite poet.

Reading this book is like crossing a long distance; turning pages is like stopping at important stages, or like slowly navigating a river before reaching the other side. You embark on a journey with this book, and when it ends, you will know that you have understood Sufism in a deeper way.

So, embark with us on this spiritual journey. Traverse the distance without hurrying, pause to ponder the meanings of the dialogue between Nasr and myself. Read verses from Rumi to Hafez, from Ibn al-Farid to Attar. You will often come across the terms "sacred" and "desacralized." The more you advance in your reading the more you will come to realize that humanity's first and foremost goal should be to save the environment before it is too late.

These discussions flow organically. It is in the nature of our dialogue to inquire, correct, clarify, and revisit. The originality of this dialogue lies in offering a comprehensive and nuanced picture of Sufism, a subject that is treated here in six different chapters, each focusing on one specific Sufi theme. However, these themes often intertwine, without being repetitive, creating an overarching unity to the whole. The discussions illuminate the correspondences that exist between Sufism and creativity, cosmology, environment, poetry, and art. The last chapter on modernity reveals how and why Sufis decry the misdeeds of modernity.

This is an important book. Nasr told me one day that "I have said things in this book that aren't present in my other works." These discussions cast light on the centrality of Sufism in Nasr's work. In his reply to Leonard Lewisohn, Nasr writes, "Whatever I have written, whether it be in the field of religion, philosophy, science, or art, has been from the perspective of Sufism in its most universal sense, which is none other than the *sophia perennis* expressed in the language of the Islamic tradition."[1]

Sufism and Creativity

Chapter 1 sheds light on the "synthesizing power" of Sufism that is due to its universal and inward character and to *ma'rifah*, or Islamic gnosis, that characterizes Sufism. It is Sufism's synthesizing force that was behind the creative incorporation of all that confirmed "its doctrine of unity."

Because of this feature, Sufism was able to integrate Pythagorean doctrines, Platonism, Neoplatonism, the ancient religions of Persia, Hinduism, and Greco-Alexandrian antiquity, which is a testimony to its inclusiveness. There is also the fact that, because Sufism belongs to the *Sophia Perennis*, it naturally finds primary resemblances in various mystical experiences across religions, cultures, and eras as well as similar rituals and sacred performances. Finally, Islam being the last celestial religion, it easily absorbed what preceded it. But there is also an important element for this most creative synthesis, which Nasr elucidates in these terms: "But if one concentrates on the Supreme Reality, which for us is Allah, the One, who is above every determination, then what 'flows' from the One is much easier to integrate within that perspective. These are very subtle, metaphysical qualities of the Islamic revelation, but on the actual level of history you can see that they enabled the Muslims to integrate into their worldview so much that had existed before Islam" (chapter 2).

Nasr has expounded on this "One single Divine Principle" in many works. Thus, in *The Need for a Sacred Science*, he writes that "the unity to which the traditionalists refer is, properly speaking, a transcendental unity above and beyond forms and external manifestations."[2] In his reply to Ernest Wolf-Gazo, he asserts that "I would say that in my case the principle of unity must also be included as an absolutely essential element of every aspect of my thought."[3]

From the perspective of Nasr, understanding the Oneness of God leads ultimately to the doctrine of *wahdat al-wujud* (Unity of Being). He reiterated in multiple instances during our dialogue that *wahdat al-wujud* is Sufism's most important pillar. It signifies that that there can be ultimately only one Reality, which is expressed in the first *shahada*, as he claims. Nasr has previously highlighted this doctrine in multiple works. In his *An Introduction to Islamic Cosmological Doctrines*, he wrote, "This formula which is the Quranic basis of the Sufi doctrine of the Unity of Being (*wahdat al-wujud*) does not imply that there is a substantial continuity between

God and the world, or any form of pantheism or monism; rather, it means that there cannot be two orders of reality independent of each other."[4]

Sufism and Cosmology

Chapter 2 on cosmology, which is also the densest, takes us on a journey across the vastness of the cosmos, whose mysteries remain enigmatic to the human mind. The dialogue between Nasr and myself stresses in many instances the "cosmic dimension" of human beings that is present throughout his work. Most importantly, Nasr reiterates that cosmology is first and foremost a sacred science rooted in metaphysical principles and revelation and ingrained in the hierarchy of a reality whose different ontological degrees correspond to different degrees of our human consciousness. Traditional cosmology elevates us to a spiritual level, as Nasr maintains: "So, spiritualization is also related to cosmology in the journey to the Beyond."

It is in this context that Nasr rejects modern Western cosmology because it reduces the cosmos to the psychophysical dimension which does not account for our cosmic origins. For him, Western cosmology cannot be completely true, because it ignores metaphysical principles.[5] Despite all these differences, Nasr maintains, "Sometimes, ideas in modern Western cosmology echo some traditional ideas, but without the metaphysical depth."

A true cosmology, henceforth, increases our self-awareness and our self-knowledge, for the cosmos is our teacher. The cosmos is conscious, as we are. The dialogue should be between two conscious realities. It is through contemplating it that we can gain a better understanding of ourselves. During our discussions, Nasr reiterated often that the laws that govern the cosmos and man are the same. The human being is, after all, the microcosm that reflects the macrocosm. Both are immersed in an incessant movement of energies, exchanges, formations, dissolutions, and reformations. The Creation is a dynamic reality made of cycles, of chaos that begets order and vice versa. It is being renewed at each moment, while human beings move with its expansion and contraction, breathing in and out like it.

The cosmos is considered in Sufism the theophany of God, and humans are invited to explore it by different means, traditional art and traditional cosmology being among them. In answer to my question about the resemblance between these two means, Nasr points out that "cosmologies are like traditional art in the sense of dealing with the multiplicity of phenomena, but always in relation to the One Divine Reality."

The Sufi, however, is neither necessarily a cosmologist nor an artist. However, his quest, which takes the form of a journey, reveals to him that the cosmos is indeed a theophany of the Divine. A great number of Sufis wrote about their journeys to the Supreme Reality. When I asked Nasr, "Why the voyage?" and whether we can do without it, he replied, "It is very simple. The reason there is a voyage, a symbolism of voyage, a wayfaring, a *sayr*, is that God is there and we are here. Metaphysically, we are already 'in God,' *fi 'Llah*, but to actually reach Him requires a voyage, a *sayr ila 'Llah* and ultimately *fi'Llah* which in most cases requires journeying through the angelic realms."

To come near the Divine, one needs to experience in his soul and body the predicament of being on earth while seeking the Absolute. Hence the exigency of the voyage. In this context, it is worth mentioning that several Sufis imitated the Prophet's ascension, *mi'raj*, and experienced in their souls and hearts the mystical voyage to the Source for a short time.

I asked Nasr why we can't read the cosmic book, since we have the *fitrah* (innate nature) in us. He mentions the need for us to remember in order to read this book. In his own words, "The cosmos that God created is a paradisiacal reality; in a sense, it is still here. It is we who are absent from it because of our faults of forgetfulness and negligence."

Sufism and Environment

Chapter 3 takes us to the question that has preoccupied Nasr greatly. He once wrote that "nothing is more important and worthy of consideration today than the environmental crisis."[6]

In the perennialist school and beyond, Nasr remains, without doubt, the philosopher who has delved the most into the crisis of the environment and who has alerted us early to the gravity of the situation.

Since the sixties of last century, Nasr has devoted a large part of his time and thought to this question. Among his numerous works, *Religion and the Order of Nature* remains in my eyes the book that encapsulates most completely his thoughts on this question. Obviously, Nasr discusses the causes of our alienation from nature in many of his other works, especially in *Man and Nature*. However, it is in *Religion and the Order of Nature* that one finds the most compelling analysis of why and how Western man gradually polluted the environment. This work was the major incentive behind the idea of this book. I was eager to discuss with him his assertion that "the loss of sapiential knowledge of nature has led us to the current disaster."[7] I was intrigued to listen to him expanding on his statement that "the desacralization of knowledge was related directly to the desacralization of the cosmos."[8]

Elsewhere, Nasr has stated that the pollution of the environment is simply the consequence of the pollution of the human soul, which has eliminated the transcendental dimension from its existence.[9] For him, human beings fail to recall their sacred origins and who they are. They have omitted from their lives "the extra-spatial and extra-temporal character."[10]

These ideas lead to a profound reevaluation of our relationship with the world. It reminds us that the human intellect partakes of divine Intelligence; that our human intelligence is joined to the Divine in such a way that what it produces has its origin in this Divine. For Nasr, it is impossible to look for solutions for our environmental crisis outside metaphysics, which is overwhelmingly present in what he terms "the religious understanding of the order of nature." As the discussion unfolds in this book, it is obvious that, for the author of *Man and Nature* and other books on the question of the environment, there is no redeeming of ourselves and of nature if we persist in ignoring the sacredness of both humans and the universe. When humanity forgot this dimension, it thought that man is the measure of everything and the ultimate master who has the right to plunder nature.

I asked Nasr if "a better understanding of nature perceived as God's theophany could help us better grasp the transcendental unity of religions." I had in mind that such an understanding might help us resolve the question of the environment. Nasr maintained that despite the fact religions differ externally, they still look at nature in their inner teachings from "a spiritual perspective."

I remembered while listening to him that he also examined this question in *Sufi Essays*, where he avers that the Chinese and Indian traditions are obvious examples of civilizations that linked nature to metaphysics. He also asserts that these traditions "study nature as a domain that is 'contained and embraced' by a supra-sensible world that is immensely greater than it."[11]

The dialogue between Nasr and me unveils seminal nuances about humanity and nature that do not occur to us usually. For example, Nasr's assertion that nature does not participate entirely in man's fall aroused my curiosity;

so I asked him to elaborate. He explained that the reason is that nature still retains its innocence because it has no free will like us and it is submitted to the Creator. That's why it still reflects its prototype that is Paradise.

Nasr, however, does not only uncover the causes that created the environmental predicament but he also puts down a chart to help us rebuild the consonance between us and nature. This part particularly fascinated me. I was keen to know how rituals can, for example, as he suggests, bring back the lost harmony between humanity and nature. I have always related nature to contemplation, silence, and peace, but it didn't occur to me that rituals could bring back the lost harmony between us and the environment. I asked him to expand on this point. He reminded me of the traditional meaning of rituals, which are not man-made and whose objective is to stream the dialogue between this world in which we live and the spiritual world. I did not think before of rituals as means to reenergize human correspondence with the multiple levels of reality. Nasr stressed one particular point that rituals should also be performed by the whole community and not by the individual alone, in the manner of the Native Americans whose collective ceremonies, like the Sun Dance, are meant to regain the lost grace and the conversation with Nature and the Great Spirit. Communal and ritualistic dances, aim to reestablish these correspondences of which Nasr speaks and make us conscious of being part of this earth that nurtures us and this cosmos. As Lame Deer avers, "We . . . also know that, being a living part of the earth, we cannot harm any part of her without hurting ourselves."[12]

In a way, rituals are connectors between us and the Divine and between us and the cosmos. I surmise that very few people today can claim that they look at rituals from this perspective. For them, performing a ritual is simply a duty that their respective religions request them to do.

This is one of the major reasons behind the gradual death of our spiritual life.

There is another way to restore the lost bond with nature, which is to resuscitate sacred science, which we discuss in the second chapter. Nasr dwells on it in his book *The Need for a Sacred Science*. In our discussions, he mentions the urgency to return to the traditional Islamic sciences and to those of India and the Far East. Most importantly, he calls upon us to reintroduce metaphysics into science or, as he says, "That is why I have always said that in order for modern civilization to survive, you have to reintegrate the modern sciences into a metaphysical perspective, which has not as yet been done in mainstream Western science."

The task that Nasr invites us to undertake is no less than reconciling ourselves with Heaven if we are serious about saving nature and ourselves.

Sufism and Poetry

As the title indicates, chapter 4 focuses on the relation between poetry and Sufism. Poetry is central in Sufism in general and in Nasr's scholarly work in particular. It is worth mentioning here that Nasr himself writes poetry and has published two anthologies of great beauty and depth, one entitled *Poems of the Way*. When I asked Nasr, alluding to that title, to clarify which way he meant, he replied that he is referring to the symbolism of spiritual wayfaring and also to honor the famous Sufi poet Ibn al-Farid (d. 1234).

Numerous are the Sufis who composed poetry, from Rabi'a al-Adwiyyah (d. 801) to al-Husayn ibn Mansour al-Hallaj (d. 922), to Ibn al-Farid, Farid al-Din Attar (d. 1221), and Jalal al-Din Rumi (d. 1273), to name just a few. As a poet myself, I was intrigued by the plethora of verse among Sufis and asked Nasr about it. His response encapsulates marvelously the link between poetry and Sufism in these terms: "Poetry is the language of the world of the Spirit" (chapter 1). Furthermore, he adds that "the Sufi poets were the channel through which metaphysical and spiritual realities were flowing into the human order."

They had, undoubtedly, access to a higher level of reality that extends beyond the phenomenal world. The visions they perceive are transmuted into words and rhythms, which takes us to the origin of things. It is interesting that many Sufi poets claim that they wrote poems in one instance as if it were an urgency to put them down. It is the divine inspiration that descends upon them. Mahmud Shabistari is a great example, as mentioned in the chapter; Ibn al-Farid is another. Other Sufi poets, like Farid al-Din Attar and Jalal al-Din Rumi, revealed that they didn't choose to write poetry. Ibn Arabi also claimed that his writing came from a sacred source. He noted, "I have not written a single letter of this book except under the influence of divine dictation."[13]

Across traditions, one finds that poetry comes from a spiritual source. One is reminded in this instance of the Ramayana in Hinduism. Valmiki, the poet who committed them to paper, claimed that it was Brahma himself who enjoined him to compose them. Sacred books, in general, were also written in verse.

Sufi poetry activates our *fitra* and rekindles our memory. We begin to remember the spiritual realms previously forgotten and we become voyagers, as Rumi says: "Remembrance makes people desire the journey; it makes them into travelers."[14] With Sufi poetry, we are on sacred grounds and as if praying in a temple. In this context, Nasr mentions one aspect of Sufi poetry that we don't think of usually, which is the continuity between poetry and religious performances. He maintains that, "in fact, a great deal of traditional poetry may be considered as a kind of prolongation of the fundamental spiritual practices of the tradition in question."[15] In Rumi's verse, for example, one finds invocations and litanies that are akin to *dhikr* and other Sufi ceremonies. The rhythms and repeated sounds used in his verse could correspond to the sounds found in sacred languages such as the *mantras* in Sanskrit, *Japa* in Hinduism, or the *Nembutsu* in Pure Land Buddhism. Commenting on Rumi's poetry, Nasr writes that "many verses, especially in the *Diwan*, induce a state of ecstasy in the trained listener by the sheer beauty of their imagery and their rhymes and rhythms."[16]

When I asked Nasr if he agrees with Annemarie Schimmel that Sufi poetry is a "quranization of the memory," he replied that he would call Sufi poetry "crystallizations of truths of the inner meanings of the Qur'an and *Hadith*." In addition to being inspired by a divine power, Sufi poetry is nurtured by the Intellect, that central faculty in the human being that alone comprehends the highest metaphysical matters and then relays them directly from the Source. The intellect is "the eye of the soul," as perennialists like to say. It recalls sacred symbols that remind us of our celestial origins. Rumi is without doubt the most obvious example of a poet who succeeded in penetrating the *ma'na*, or meaning, that lies beyond the *surah*, or form. As Nasr avers, "For Rumi, all things are symbols revealing the spiritual worlds above; all forms are symbols which in his eyes, as in the eyes of all gnostics, become transparent, revealing the 'meaning' beyond."[17]

William Chittick, in turn, sums up beautifully the task of Sufi poetry in these terms: "The positive role that poetry can play is to awaken the imaginal perception of God's Self-disclosures."[18]

Sufi poetry flows beyond time and place. Maybe that's why we feel that we entered eternity during the short time of reading or reciting it. Nasr cites Rumi as someone who still draws a lot of interest, especially in America, because the message he brings is timeless.

One of the very important points that we discussed in this chapter was the triangle of music, poetry, and silence. Being inspired by the Divine, Sufi poetry not only molds its language in accordance with the world of the Spirit, but also it molds its music, which the higher realms confer to it. Nasr reminded me that "Sufi poetry, great Sufi poetry, is inseparable from music. Much of it is actually combined with the playing of music, because in the *sama*, in the *majalis* of the Sufis, music and Sufi poetry go hand in hand."

Once again, Nasr gives the example of Rumi as someone whose poetry is carried on the wings of music; you cannot read it without also singing it, he tells me. Some Sufis do not need *sama*, simply because they are attuned to the divine music that is beyond any form of music humans can create. In this context, we discussed what has been called "silent music," or "pure inner music," as Henry Corbin describes it when evoking Ruzbihan Baqli's treatise on music.

As often in this book, our dialogue went beyond the questions asked and the responses provided. This is exactly what interested me the most in our dialogue. For example, once we almost exhausted the relation of poetry and music, the discussion turned to a much larger kind of "silent music." When I asked Nasr about the music of the celestial spheres, I was fascinated by his answer. Thus, the discussion moved from the relation of poetry to music to something much larger and deeper: the relation of poetry to mathematics and astronomy. First, Nasr maintained that, "according to the Pythagorean doctrine, the planetary system is also based on music in its relation to mathematics." It was extremely interesting to learn, as Nasr maintained, that "Kepler discovered the laws of planetary motion, that is, through music and the relationality and proportionality between the movement of the various planets and their distance from the sun or earth and so forth. Kepler was dealing in a sense with musical numbers." In this context, the figures of Ikhwan al-Safa', al-Farabi, and Ibn Sina were evoked as philosophers who examined the link that connects metaphysics to traditional sciences and music.

Art and Sufism

Chapter 5 unveils the central role that arts in general play in Islamic mysticism. In answer to my question whether Sufism can grow without the arts, Nasr stressed that it cannot, despite the desire of Sufis to transcend "the formal order as the goal of the path." There is only one exception: if a Sufi attains the state of *fana'* (extinction in God), in which case he becomes himself the supreme piece of art created by God, the Divine Artisan.

Then the conversation moved to the symbol of the mirror, one of the most seminal symbols of Sufism, which is evoked in the writings of almost all traditionalists. Sufis wrote about it profusely. For example, Ibn Arabi maintained "that God created the mirror so that we could speak of His relation to the world." The Great Sheikh is referring here to the important notion that art in Islam is not about aesthetics and craft only, but it is also about knowledge. The truth that one finds in Islamic art is reached through the intellect and not through reason. Ananda Coomaraswamy looked at the artist as a priest performing a ministerial function and at sacred art not as an aesthetic object, but rather "as an intellectual virtue and beauty as pertaining to knowledge."[19]

While I suggested that the mirror is an expression of the relation between form and essence, Nasr went further, unraveling deeper the meanings inherent in the symbol of the mirror by asserting that the mirror "is, in a sense, the relation of the archetype to its earthly reflection." Similarly, Titus Burkhardt found that the mirror represents a "union of subject and object."[20]

The dialogue in this chapter treats complex and profound ideas. Three main points were discussed. The first one is the relation between mathematics and metaphysics. While listening to Nasr expand on this relation, I remembered having read in *Man and Nature* that the author maintains that both metaphysics and mathematics are rigorous sciences having the same precision and reliability.[21] For Nasr, metaphysics and mathematics meet in sacred art, especially in poetry, which with logic, refers to the same Reality. In his response to Leonard Lewisohn, Nasr maintained that "I have often written that poetry and mathematics can meet and have a common ground only in gnosis which possesses both the rigor of mathematics and the beauty of poetry."[22]

The second point we tackled revolved around sonoral arts and visual arts. I asked Nasr which of these arts is closer to the the *haqiqah qur'aniyyah* (the truth of the Qur'an). He responded that the sonoral art is "the central Islamic art" because "the Qur'an was before anything else a sonoral revelation before being written down."

The third question revolved around the seminal relation in art between being and seeing. Nasr stressed that sacred art transforms our being, because it isn't only about the imagination of an individual. "It is based upon principles which relate it to the cosmos; so, in beholding it you feel to be at the center of the cosmos."

In fact, it is unbelievable how, when contemplating a piece of art, one is swiftly seized by the remembrance of the Divine. Traditional art has the power by its beauty and harmony to awaken us to Reality and brings back to us the souvenir of the Origins. As Huston Smith sums it up so well, "If one is viewing an icon (in a way, all sacred art is iconic), then the icon basically disappears by offering itself up to the Divine. The energy of the Divine pours through it into the viewer, one consequence being that the viewer's heart is expanded and becomes uplifted by a great work of art."[23]

In this chapter as in others, Islamic art is compared to other arts in other traditions, such as the concept of the void in Islamic art, Buddhist art, and Taoism, and the place of Pythagoras in Islam and in Christianity.

Finally, in our discussion of the symbol, we delved into the union of symbol and symbolized that some primal people still hold. Great art does not only evoke the Divine, but also, and by the same token, represents symbolically eternity in time.

Sufism and Modernity

The final chapter deals with the ugliness of the modern world. Nasr, adamantly criticizes modernism in all its manifestations. He maintains that he was profoundly influenced by the works of the Traditionalist masters who preceded him and who wrote on modernity, such as René Guénon (d. 1951), Ananda Coomaraswamy (d. 1947), and Frithjof Schuon (d. 1998). Like them, he believes that modern and postmodern philosophy have chosen a path that can only lead to our demise. Many among us fear the consequences of modernism, which brought incoherence, vanity, and purposelessness in our lives. We sense the coming catastrophe, and profoundly dread seeing our future annihilation unless a miracle happens. We realize with stupefaction that, for the first time in human history, logos and mythos have parted ways, while they had remained complimentary until now. This is ushering in the loss of a true spirituality.

When I asked Nasr about the difference between the works of his predecessors and his own, he mentioned that it is his "extensive critiques of modern science in relation to religion."[24] That's why he is eager to bring back sacred science that is based on metaphysical principles and centered most and foremost on the nature of Reality.

Nasr is recognized as being also the first traditionalist to study the crisis of the environment, which none of his predecessors had examined. It is stunning how he looks at this crisis from different angles. For example, he attributes the breaking of the social fabric to the rise of a ferocious individualism and the sacralization of history. Time is seen as linear, represented by an arrow, while it is cyclic in traditionalist thinking. He encapsulates the consequences in these terms: "The deification of historical process has become so powerful and such a compelling force that, in the souls of many human beings, it has taken the place of religion."[25] The consequences of modernism are prominent, not only in science and thought, but also in art. The result is a disfiguration of the human soul and its environment, thus creating an ugly space where we move and think without having a center.

One of the examples of disfiguration is the elimination of the sacramental aspect of Islamic art. He gives the example of Islamic architecture today in the urban places in the Islamic world, asserting that "the atrocious destruction of so much Islamic architecture and even of sanctuaries and holy cities by apparently devout Muslims is proof, if proof is necessary, of the significance of the loss of that Divine wisdom that contains the principles of Islamic art."[26]

Such a situation has led to the burgeoning of movements such as the New Age movement and other movements that have become very popular. Nasr argues that, if no spiritual awakening appears on the horizon, these movements will become stronger, because they fill a vacuum left by the absence of the sacred from the lives of many people.

Toward the end of this chapter, we discussed the role of prayer in the modern world. Then the conversation branched spontaneously to the resemblances between Hinduism and

Islam, two religions that make no difference between sacred and profane and whose adepts continue to perform their rituals in the midst of secularism and scientism.

Although I had assigned to each chapter its central theme and around which the conversation would proceed naturally, I would find myself spontaneously diverting from the central theme of a chapter and setting the dialogue from a different angle without breaking the natural flow of the discussion. For example, in the chapter on poetry, when discussing Nasr's use of different pronouns to evoke the Divine in his mystical poetry, the conversation slowly shifted to profound metaphysical issues such as the relation between the I and the One.

Last but not least, this book unveils Nasr's opinions regarding many important intellectual and scientific figures of the twentieth century, such as Henry Corbin, Louis Massignon, Martin Heidegger, Ásin Palacios, Joseph Campbell, Carl Gustave Jung, Mircea Eliade, Fritjof Capra, and Carl Sagan, among others. It is a trove inasmuch as Nasr sheds light on his personal relationships with many of them and reveals these thinkers' stands on a range of issues that were discussed in this book, such as religion and the sacred, mythology and mysticism, science and faith, Sufism and modernity, and resemblances and differences between traditions, especially between Islam and Christianity and between Islam and Hinduism.

Chapter 1

Sufism and Creativity

EL-ZEIN: Suppose I am a Westerner. I hear people around me talking about Sufism, and I am curious. I want to know about it, and I come to you and I ask, What is Sufism?

NASR: Sufism is a path which leads us to God, the highest meaning of the term God being both the personal God and the Godhead or Ultimate Reality. And since all authentic spiritual paths must be within the world created by Revelation, which is the manifestation of the Divine through the Logos, the path must be within an orthodox framework of religion. Sufism is such a path within Islam.

EL-ZEIN: So you think that Sufism has its own Islamic grassroots?

NASR: Absolutely. Sufism is based on three elements. First of all, it is based on the truth that is contained within the Noble Qur'an, the inner dimension of the Qur'an, the inner meaning of the Qur'an, the *haqiqah* (truth) that is contained within the Qur'an, which comes from God. The second element is the example of the blessed Prophet Muhammad and the virtues, which were perfected within the being of the Prophet, owing to the fact that he was the last Prophet of God, the perfect model to be followed by all Muslims. The third element is the spiritual power and influence, which is called *al-barakah al-muhamadiyyah* (the Muhammadan grace). It is a very distinctive spiritual current issuing from the inner reality of the Prophet, and is metaphorically speaking like the energy which makes possible for a lamp to become lit and emanate light, or spiritual reality that makes possible, in fact, the very practice of Sufism. All of these three elements spring directly from the Islamic Revelation, and they are the foundations of Sufism.

EL-ZEIN: Here, I think of the great Persian Sufis, such as Suhrawardi, 'Attar, Hafiz. And I think mainly of Corbin's interpretation of Suhrawardi. I am referring here specifically to his astonishing work, *L'homme de lumière dans le soufisme iranien*, where he shows that Suhrawardi made an extraordinary synthesis between Zoroastrianism as an old religion of Persia and Neoplatonism. As for the *Hadith* and the Qur'an, it seems to be only in the background. Do you think that Corbin went too far in his interpretation of Suhrawardi?

NASR: Corbin and I were friends for many years and were close collaborators. We taught seminars together on Islamic philosophy and Sufism at Tehran University for twenty years. He wrote some of the most brilliant books on Sufism, and I have a lot of respect for his work. As for his interpretation of the synthesis carried by Suhrawardi, it does not negate what I am saying about the origin of Sufism at all! Because you must understand that this synthesis, carried out by a person like Suhrawardi and some other people in Persia, has for its basis and framework Islamic metaphysical teachings. Pre-Islamic teachings chosen by Suhrawardi do not invalidate the Qur'anic doctrines. The Qur'an in fact provides the very universal perspective that had made such syntheses possible.

The knowledge that made possible such a synthesis as that of Suhrawardi and which enabled him to carry out such a path is Islamic gnosis or *ma'rifah*, Islamic divine knowledge which comes precisely from the Qur'an and the

Hadith. It may at first appear that Qur'an and *Hadith* are only in the background, as you mention. But such is not the truth. The exterior form of the Qur'an and *Hadith* are the point of departure, you might say, for the penetration into the inner meaning of the sacred text and the teachings of the Prophet, peace and blessings be upon Him. But that inner meaning itself does not imply that the outer meaning was redundant and is irrelevant. The inward cannot be reached except by means of the outward.

Why is it that Suhrawardi did not bring into being another philosophy outside the Islamic tradition? We have a similar situation in the Christian civilization, with Saint Augustine. Why is it that Saint Augustine read Plato and integrated Plato into the Christian perspective and did not treat it independent of Christianity? It is by virtue of the possibilities inherent within the Christian tradition that Saint Augustine was enabled to do what he did, namely, to formulate Christian Platonism. He did not become less Christian by doing so. The same truth holds for Suhrawardi and other Islamic figures like him in their approach to philosophy.

There is also another point, which is absolutely essential: Islam is the last plenary revelation of our human history, and, as a result of this finality, it contains a very great power of synthesis and integration of what came before it. Islam considers the truth not to be unique to itself, in contrast to many other religions, but to have been revealed through other prophets throughout history. Even the word Islam does not begin in the Qur'an with the Prophet Muhammad. The prophets Abraham and Jesus are called Muslim in Islam's sacred text. Yet they lived thousands of years before the advent of the Qur'anic Revelation in the year 610 when the first *surah* (chapter) was revealed to the Prophet Muhammad by the Archangel Gabriel in Makkah.

Because of this synthesis, Islam sees everything, which confirms its doctrine of Unity, of *tawhid*, as being Islamic in the deepest sense. Now, precisely since Sufism is that aspect of Islam which deals with the most universal and the most inward reality—because the inward and the universal go together in contrast to the outer and the particular—the synthesizing power of Islam is manifested mostly in Sufism.

In India, Sufism encountered Hinduism and certain forms of Buddhism. In Syria, it encountered Christian spirituality. In Persia, it encountered Zoroastrian doctrines and Manichaeism. Sufis did not look at the inner meanings of these religions as anti-Islamic. They tried to see what they were in essence, and they never adopted elements which were against the Islamic point of view. Suhrawardi himself was very clear on this issue when he said that he was against dualism *thuna'iyyah,* and when he praised the ancient wisdom of the Persians, he was talking about the sages among the Persians who were among the *muwahidun,* who were unitarians. The Sufis did not accept elements which were against the Islamic perspective, such as outward polytheism, or dualism, as in the case of the classical interpretation of Zoroastrianism. But when they met doctrines or languages or in particular symbolism which was in accordance with the perspective of Islam, which the Sufis tried to realize at the highest level, they sometimes integrated these elements into their teachings, which must not be confused with turning their backs upon the Qur'an.

EL-ZEIN: I agree with you. But while I, like you, understand Suhrawardi from this perspective, I think that Corbin focused on the fact that Suhrawardi wanted to revive the pre-Islamic heritage of Persia.

NASR: This is a very specific issue to which you are alluding. Corbin was not a Sufi, although he had a great love for Sufism. Corbin had a kind of existential "participation" in the Islamic universe. Let me put it this way: He was very close to the *Shi'ah* point of view, even though he was not practicing *Shi'ism.* His participation was mostly intellectual, but of a high order.

What Corbin was interested in with the specific work that you are mentioning, and in other books as well, was the resuscitation of Persian myths and metaphysical and philosophical doctrines in the Islamic period, and there is something profound, no doubt, in this search! Louis Massignon, the teacher of Corbin, once said that "Islam was the mirror in which Iran contemplated many of its ancient myths."

In fact, it was by virtue of the esoteric dimension of Islam that Islamic Persia was able to integrate its past into its culture. Had there been only the externalized forms of Islam, such integration would not have been possible! But this integration did not negate the external elements of Islam. Suhrawardi lived at a time when Islam had already spread all over Persia centuries ago, and he practiced Islam when he went to the mosque and when he prayed as the Persians still do eight hundred years after him.

EL-ZEIN: I want to come back to this fascinating issue: Islam as a synthesis. It seems to me that Suhrawardi did his own creative synthesis. He integrated Neoplatonism into Zoroastrianism—without accepting the dualism of the latter—and enveloped the whole integration within the Islamic tradition. He made the theme of Light the center of his work. With him, Light is not in battle with the darkness as in classical Zoroastrianism. God is Light, as the Qur'an tells us.

NASR: That is right. The Qur'an says: "God is the light of heavens and the earth" (24: 35). Suhrawardi refers to God as *nur al-anwar* (the Light of lights). What Suhrawardi did was to adopt the language of Mazdean angelology and synthesize it with the theses of Neoplatonism. He created a metaphysical language based on the symbolism of light in a very powerful way and there is no doubt that he was a great "genius" intellectually speaking.

But you must understand that both Neoplatonism and the elements of the Mazdean and Zorastrian tradition which he adopts for his doctrines all involve the metaphysical language and must not be confused with the experiential aspect of the world of the Spirit which was made possible for him only through Islamic esoterism. We must not forget that Sufism is based on a way that leads to the experience of the Divine. All Sufi doctrine is a language erected to describe the path leading to that experience and contains signposts on the path of direct knowledge. The intellection that accompanies the following of the spiritual path leads to divine knowledge, Islam being a way of sapiental realization. Islam is a religion of knowledge and also possesses a gnostic form of mysticism, and I mean "mysticism" in its authentic sense. Islamic mysticism or Sufism is essentially a sapiental one. Therefore, the language used to describe its inner truth can be drawn from other metaphysical systems, which are cogent and pertinent as long as they possess the appropriate language. For Western civilization, the intellectual language of mysticism was essentially provided by Platonism and Neoplatonism. The deepest mystical Christian writings, such as the *Celestial Hierarchies* of Dionysius, are all dressed in a language drawn from Platonism and Neoplatonism, but what made the Christian mystical experience possible was not Greek philosophy; it was Christ and the grace of Christianity.

In studying Platonism and Neoplatonism, modern scholarship often confuses the language with the reality. There was a language drawn from Graeco-Alexandrian sources that was used by Islamic as well as Christian mysticism, whose mysticism is, however, based more on love than knowledge, for a spiritual reality that comes from the origin of the religion in question. The Christian case is similar to that of Islam, except that Islam had more access to diverse mystical traditions and languages than Christianity, because Islam not only inherited the metaphysical teachings of the Greco-Alexandrian antiquity as we also see in Christian civilization, but also the Persian and sometimes the Eastern traditions, such as those of India and China with which early Christianity had no contact and about which the West had heard little until modern times.

EL-ZEIN: You speak of Sufism integrating many metaphysical languages. I want to raise with you the issue of Sufism integrating poetical languages in addition to metaphysical ones. It seems to me that Sufism is not only a synthesis on the plane of ideas and languages, but also on the plane of forms. Sufis wrote in all forms, in all genres, from the essay to the story to the poem. . . . I am alluding here to the extraordinary power of creativity within Sufism. And I have in mind specifically the wonderful *Mawaqif* (Stations) of Niffari.

My question is, how can we link this creativity on all planes to the issue of modernity, which asserts that we are in an age which surpasses all forms and goes beyond all genres? Were not Sufis already doing this a long time ago?

NASR: All synthesis is based on creativity. But the question you are alluding to has several dimensions. First of all, the power of creation of forms in Sufism is very different from what is being done in what is called "modernity" in the world today, because what people are trying to do in the modern world has no access to the world beyond forms. They break forms from below, whereas a form in a spiritual sense is like the outer shell of a walnut or of a pistachio, which is necessary to protect the kernel within it.

Sufis had access to what Mawlana Jalal al-Din Rumi calls *ma'na* (meaning) in contrast to *surah* (form). *Surah* is not used here in the Aristotelian sense, but as the external form, and *ma'na* as the inner meaning, the inner reality. The Sufi, by virtue of reaching the world of *ma'na*, of inner meaning, is freed from above from the constraints of external forms. All authentic creativity in traditional civilization takes place in this way; that is, the reality of what is to be created originates in the world of the formless, and as it enters into formal manifestation, it also enters the world of forms.

It is important to note that in the modern world experimentation with forms in literature, painting, art, and music, et cetera, means breaking away from tradition! Tradition is seen only negatively by the modern mind as being a constraint. To be modern means to break away from tradition and seek to create one's own forms. There is always something very individualistic in this outlook and in what is called "creativity" which is very different from creativity in a traditional civilization.

Perhaps the best example of liberation from all known forms is—as you mentioned—the *Mawaqif* of Niffari and, in Persian, the ecstatic poems of Mawlana Jalal al-Din Rumi in his *Grand Diwan*. When you listen to these poems, they are unbelievably ecstatic and break all the norms of prosody used at that time.

But the creativity of both Niffari and Rumi is very different from some contemporary Persian or Arab poets who are trying to emulate Western poetry and so break the traditional poetic forms. In Arabic you have what is called *al-shi'r al-hurr* (free verse) which should not be confused with the Sufi freedom from forms. The creativity of the great Sufis does not come from a foreign model or the ego center. There is not a need to express the individual, to express what I call "myself." The Sufis have already gone beyond the "self" and have reached the Universal Reality. They teach from the "heart intellect," the "divine center" of our being which is the origin of all forms and the archetypal world.

Of course, there is always the imprint of the genius who invented these forms, but this does not mean only an individualistic expression, which is why one observes this continuity in the Sufi tradition that one does not see in the modern Western world.

You may have a great genius like Michelangelo or a great poet like John Keats, but they do not mark a continuous tradition. They disappear and then after a while you have another genius, another star.

Rumi, who lived eight hundred years ago, is much more alive in Iran today than any nineteenth-century great English poet is in England. So creativity, yes, but creativity which comes from interiority, from inwardness; and the synthesis which you mentioned is not only "intellectual" in the ordinary sense or artistic. It is a synthesis which has definitely to do with the Sufi's access to the higher levels of Reality.

EL-ZEIN: Could you elaborate more on what you just said, that Rumi is much more alive in Iran today than any English poet of the nineteenth century is in England? Why is it so, do you think?

NASR: First of all, the West continues to be what I call an "anti-traditional" civilization, a civilization no longer based on abiding principles. This anti-traditional civilization began in the Renaissance but something of the traditional Middle Ages survived in Elizabethan England. This continuity can be found in the work of Shakespeare in England with its deeper meaning being closely akin to the work of Dante in Italy. These two poets are very much alive today precisely because their works contain elements of tradition and therefore timeless truth. But what we see today in Western Europe and in America is an anti-traditional civilization, which means that every generation feels that it has to turn against perennial truth and preceding generations in order to express itself and be "creative" and original.

The reason for the continuous popularity of Rumi today is that he is speaking from and about the realities that are timeless. Writers today choose to be timely, so timely as to soon become irrelevant—that is the heart of the matter. Rumi does not speak of external things which change, but of the abiding truth that we contain within ourselves, of metaphysical realities, of our journey through this world where we encounter certain problems, needs, nostalgias, experiences of love, withdrawal, and intimations of death and immortality, et cetera, which continue to challenge us. If he had spoken only of the Anatolia of the thirteenth century, today he would have been interesting only to historians of Anatolia.

A person such as Rumi elaborated the thesis that we are in this world for a purpose: that we have come from God and we must return to God. And the great questions as well as truths are discovered when you realize this ultimate Reality. I would say that, from the point of view of a person such as Rumi, most of the questions which are posed today in the domain of philosophy, religion and spirituality are ill-posed questions, and so we try to provide answers to wrong questions.

I would like to mention here that not only the Sufis within Islam spoke of the eternal truths, but also the Islamic philosophers. Suhrawardi was himself both a Sufi and a philosopher at the same time, which constitute two distinct schools in Islam, although sometimes synthesized.

The idea of "perennial philosophy"—which is now becoming somewhat popular in the West—goes back to a statement made by a librarian in the Vatican in the sixteenth century, Augustino Steuco, who coined the term *Philosophia Perennis*. But that idea had already been well-known in the Islamic world long before Steuco. For Sufis and Islamic philosophers, truth is timeless and is like gold, which does not rust with time. Truth belongs to eternal *Sophia*. That is why, long before Steuco, Islamic philosophers such as Ibn Miskawayh spoke of *Philosophia Perennis* (*al-hikmah al-khalidah* or *jawidan-khirad*). In fact, maybe we should use *Sophia Perennis* rather than *Philosophia Perennis*, for on the highest level this *Sophia* was promulgated by the Prophet with the rise of Islam, having been resuscitated with the Islamic Revelation. It is this Sophia to which the Qur'an refers as *al-din al-hanif* (primordial monotheism). Someone like Rumi not only tried to speak of this Sophia, but succeeded in doing so in the most eloquent of terms. That is why he speaks to even many Americans much more directly than do contemporary American poets.

EL-ZEIN: I want to go back to this issue of creativity in Sufism. You mentioned that creativity in Sufism is always linked to tradition, while modern poetry is not linked to tradition. But there is something fascinating about modern poetry, whether it be Western or Arab, and that is the fact that modern poetry, contrary to what you say, wants to re-source itself by going back to tradition. I would like to go back to surrealism, for example. In his first manifesto, André Breton, one of the founders of the surrealist movement, asserted that surrealism takes its inspiration from mysticism. In fact, most of the surrealist poetry is impregnated with mysticism. Modern Arab poets themselves have been very influenced by this surrealistic movement. Modern Arab poetry took its inspiration from two sources in general: first, the surrealist movement with its mystic tendency, and the second very important source of inspiration being Sufism itself. My point is that modern Arab poetry is not cut off from tradition. Sufis such as al-Hallaj and al-Niffari are very popular in modern Arabic poetry today.

NASR: Yes. But one should be careful. When you say that modern poets want to go back to mysticism, what does that mean? To go back authentically to mysticism means that one must be seriously a mystic. It means to follow a genuine spiritual path (*tariqah*) and go back to God, which is what most modern Arab poets and modern Persian poets have not done.

Modern Arab poetry and modern Persian poetry (and by modern I do not mean contemporary but that which is imbued with the modernist ethos) began with the emulation of a foreign poetical form which was that of French and English, and to some extent German; languages all belonging to modern Western secularized civilization, not to a traditional foreign civilization, such as that of medieval India, whose poetry was impregnated completely by religion. Modern Arab and Persian poets were mostly influenced by the poetry of the Western world in which the poet is a lonely figure, not knowing how to fit, bewildered, full of doubt, an often sad, sometimes irrational personage. Modern Western poetry has for the most part been expelled from serious discourse about knowledge and has become separated from the sacred. It is interesting that the term *shi'r* in Arabic, which means poetry, has to do with *shu'ur* (consciousness or knowledge), whereas *poesis* has to do with "making."

EL-ZEIN: It is "techné."

NASR: Exactly. This is the Greek meaning of poetry. Poetry in medieval times was considered to be related to knowledge, as in the *Divine Comedy*. But the domain of knowledge was taken over by rationalistic philosophy, and later on by modern science; so poetry came to be simply the expression of sentiments and emotions. Romanticism tried to react against rationalistic worldview, but most romantic poets did not have the intellectual acumen and metaphysical knowledge to produce a poetry that could seriously challenge the domains of philosophy and science, which claimed for themselves exclusively the domain of knowledge. They did not have any impact upon the mainstream intellectual life of the West.

It was at this juncture that modern Arab and Persian poets encountered Western poetry. They tried to emulate both the form and even to an extent content of Western poetry. They functioned as poets but outside of the main Islamic tradition and for the most part did not have access to authentic Sufi circles, any *zawiyah* or *halaqah*. They were not practicing Sufis, or in many cases even practicing Muslims. They forgot that Arabic is a sacred language, the language of the Qur'an.

Modern Arab and Persian poets, in contrast to traditional ones, became as alienated from their societies as are the Western poet from the mainstream in Western society, although poetry remained much more alive in their cultures than in the West. Their interest—of most modern Arab and Persian poets as well as Turkish and Pakistani ones in mysticism, as you mention—was simply an individualistic and often only literal interest. They did not become serious *faqirs*! They did not lead an ascetic and contemplative life as a mystic does in Islam or for that matter Christianity. They were only attracted by the beauty of Sufi poetry and in some cases mystical Christian poetry. Few of them knew the "imaginal" world, as Corbin would say, this world which opens up in its higher reaches to the mystics, not to speak of the archetypal and intelligible worlds.

In the traditional world a poet cannot function in a living space from which the invisible world is absent. Serious poetry has to do with the imaginal and spiritual worlds. The great voices among the Western poets, such as W. B. Yeats, T. S. Eliot, and Ezra Pound, perhaps the three greatest poets of the English language during the last century, turned either to the world of mythology, as in the case of Yeats, or to the world of religion, specifically Christianity in the case of T. S. Eliot, or to Oriental poetry, especially Chinese and Persian, in the case of Pound.

Many modern Arab and Persian poets do not share a common worldview with the vast majority of their Muslim brothers and sisters. You know as well as I that many modern poets in the Islamic world are not read by even a thousand persons. You cannot take their poetry to the Khan al-Khalili bazaar in Cairo, for example, and read it to the people there, but you can take a poem of Ibn al-Farid or Busiri, which are difficult, and read them and people will come to listen. The reason is that people in the Cairo bazaar know that Ibn al-Farid is talking about their spiritual culture, while most modern Muslim poets are not.

What is the most universal poetry in Islam? It is Sufi poetry, not the poetry of Farazdaq or Jarir. As far as Arabic is concerned, it is the poetry of Ibn al-Farid, of Ibn 'Arabi, the poetry of Sheikh al-'Alawi in Algeria, whose divan has had numerous editions. As for modern Arab and Persian poetry, I believe that it is mostly unlikely that it has produced as yet a poet who will last for centuries.

Creativity comes almost always from religion, spirituality and inner vision, from the inner life. It is not accidental that the foundations of all the vernacular languages are mystical. What is the first major work in Italian? It is the canticles of Saint Francis of Assisi and the *Divine Comedy* of Dante. What is the first work of the English language? It is the *Canterbury Tales* of Chaucer, which contains the tales of religious pilgrims. What is the first work in German? It is Meister Eckhart's sermons.

This is an important lesson to learn. But in order to do so, modern Arab and Persian poets should become reintegrated into their own traditions, not only linguistically, but also spiritually.

The great Persian and Arab Sufi poets did not even claim that they were poets. They were poets despite themselves. I was teaching a course in Sufi Persian literature yesterday, and was reading the thirteenth-century mystic Farid ad-Din al-'Attar with the students. He says, "I am not a poet. Do not look at my poetry as the work of a poet. Poetry flows from me. Do not look at my prosody. Look for the meaning." This is what real poetry is!

EL-ZEIN: You mentioned that Sufi poets were much more popular than modern Arab and Persian poets because they were linked to tradition. You also mentioned that people would come in much greater number to listen to them than to listen to modern poets. My question is, Should we evaluate poetry by the number of listeners or readers?

NASR: Of course not. I agree with you that the reaction of the public is completely secondary. We have had great poets in Islamic civilization who were from the spiritual elite (*khawass*) and who were not popular, and we have had poets who were very popular and at the same time of a very high spiritual and intellectual quality. Finally, we have poets who were very popular but not of a very high spiritual quality; yet they operated within the norms of tradition. All three possibilities have existed.

In any case, we must not equate the fact that someone is very popular with the fact that his or her poetry is very profound and lasting. What makes poetry lasting is precisely the expression of lasting values which belong to the eternal world, to the world of the spirit. But the elite among traditional poets must not be compared with the modern poets who do not write for the spiritual *khawass* (elite) of their own civilization at all, although there are some exceptions.

EL-ZEIN: So, for you, lasting poetry is spiritual poetry?

NASR: Definitely. It is not only true in the case of poetry, but also of philosophy, as I mentioned before. Why is it that in the West a lot of people still read Plato rather than some of the philosophers of the eighteenth or nineteenth century, despite the fact that those later philosophers became so famous during their own days? It is because they were dealing with the transient, while Plato was dealing with the eternal.

To come back to Islam, the poets who are still famous are those who knew how to transcend their "ethnic" conditions and particularities, who spoke of universal values rather than of particular and local ones. You, as an Arab woman reading a Punjabi poet, will not be interested in his feelings toward his land, but rather in his description of the love of God, of the yearning of the soul and other universal aspects of human existence.

EL-ZEIN: What is the common boundary of Sufism and poetry? Is it the unveiling of the Invisible?

NASR: There is more to it than that. The most profound element that connects Sufism to poetry is the following:

Sufism is a way for us to peel off the outward levels or dimensions of our being, the outside skin, and to penetrate to the heart of our being. Now, through this act of penetration to the center of our being, our language is affected and becomes more interiorized. We know from anthropological and historical records that archaic people were very poetic and often spoke poetry more than prose.

In a sense if we speak in Islamic terms, we can say that Adam spoke poetry in the Garden of Eden—there is no doubt about it. The sacred Scriptures are always highly poetical, not only the Qur'an, but also the Psalms, the Upanishads, the I Ching. The reason is when the spirit of human beings, as it comes in contact with the Divine Spirit, receives from It a message imbued with the poetic art and participates in the cadences and rhythms of the spiritual world. Poetry is the language of the world of the Spirit, and therefore the Sufi message finds poetry a most suitable vehicle for the expression of its teachings more than ordinary prose. Much of even the prose works of Sufis has a poetic quality like the first chapter (*fasl*) of Ibn 'Arabi's *Fusus al-hikam*. Sufism is able to mold language in such a way as to bring out the inner meaning of things. The person who writes "authentic" Sufi poetry has recourse to words which emanate from another level of consciousness than an ordinary poet. It also addresses another level of our being; the level of dancing in front of God, always in a state in accord with the rhythmic melodies which then pour out often in the form of poetry. It is interesting that the great Sufi poets never claimed to be poets.

EL-ZEIN: Because they were so absorbed in this union with God, and with the universe, to the point that they were not aware of the poetry flowing in them through this union?

NASR: In general, yes. But let us be careful. They were not united with the universe as such. They were united with what is beyond the universe and in many cases with the manifestation of that Beyond in the cosmos. They were united with the Divine Reality, of which the universe is but a manifestation. Their poetry was the product of something other than the individual creativity that is taking place within their being. The Sufi poets were the channel through which metaphysical and spiritual realities were flowing into the human order.

EL-ZEIN: To explore these Divine Realities that you are mentioning, do you think the Sufi needs to be isolated, cut off from society? I know that you mention in your book *Sufi Essays* that "Sufism can be practiced in any circumstances in which man finds himself, in the traditional world as well as in the modern world."[1] You add further in the same page, "Since it is based on the social and juridical teachings of Islam, Sufism is meant to be practiced within society and not in a monastic environment outside the social order."[2] Do you not think that a Sufi is in exile even if he or she lives in society?

NASR: What I meant by saying "Sufism can be practiced within society" was that the Sufi can be a carpenter, a banker, a university professor, et cetera, and not live in a monastic situation, cut off from the activity of the society. Sufism is not rooted in society or outside society. Sufism is rooted in God. Therefore, the roots of the Sufi who is performing his functions in society are not in this world; they are in God. He lives in this world but is inwardly detached from it. As a Moroccan Sufi once said, "It is not I who has left the world. It is the world which has left me."

The second point you are alluding to is a very important one, which is that a spiritual person is always in exile in this world. 'Attar used to sell herbs. The fact that he was selling herbs does not mean he was a worldly person. We read in his verse that his love for God was very intense even when he was selling herbs in his drug store.

The idea of exile is a very profound theme in all of mysticism, and emphasized in Islam. We have the famous *Hadith* of the Prophet: "Islam started in exile and will return as it started; and happy are those who are in exile." This *Hadith* has been interpreted by Sufis on so many levels. A spiritual person is a *gharib* (stranger, exile) in this world.

This theme has been beautifully treated by Suhrawardi in his *Qissat al-ghurbah al-gharbiyyah* (The Tale of the Occidental Exile), which is one of the great masterpieces in philosophical mysticism in Islam. A spiritual person must feel a certain sense of "exile" in this world, which is in fact the sign of his or her sincerity toward God. But this has little to do with the manner in which he lives outwardly.

When I wrote this passage in *Sufi Essays*, I was talking about how the phenomenon of mysticism manifests itself in Islam. If you take a plane and travel to Spain, for example, you will find many Catholic monasteries. If you go to India, you will find many ashrams. People in those two places might leave their outward activities in society and go to these places to pray and contemplate, but there are no such places in Islam. A Sufi *zawiyah* is not monastery or ashram. If you go to the *bazaar* of Damascus, you might stumble upon a great Sufi sitting in his shop. There is no designated place in Islam to which you withdraw from society in an external way. The only exception is the few hermits who live in the bosom of nature away from society.

EL-ZEIN: But even in Islam, there are orders. The Sufis have their own orders.

NASR: Of course we have Sufi orders in Islam. But the members of these Sufi orders are integrated within society. If you go to a city like Cairo today, where the Sufi orders are very much alive, and you attend one of the Sufi gatherings, let us say in the mosque of al-Husayn where branches of the Shadhiliyyah Order meet regularly, you can see people participating in invocations, prayers, and chantings. Then, after the meeting, they all go home. Nearly all of them are married and some have many children. And the next morning, you might find some of those who were chanting selling sweets in a shop or working in a factory. We do have Sufi orders, but they are a society within the society and not an organization formally separated from the rest of society.

EL-ZEIN: But Sufi orders have their own rituals, and some of these rituals are very sophisticated.

NASR: Of course. If you take Sufism seriously, then that implies first of all the "rite of initiation." When you are born into a Muslim family, and your father whispers in your ears, "There is no god but God and Muhammad is his Prophet." In Christianity, we have the rite of baptism which was originally an initiation rite. One was accepted in this way into the early religious community.

Sufism is the esoteric dimension of Islam. It requires making a *bay'ah*, or initiatic pact, which has been handed down over the generations going back to the Prophet. The external rites of Sufism are the rites of Islam: prayer, fasting, Hajj, et cetera. But Sufis have also their own forms of invocation, chanting, forms of meditation which cannot be done without the power of initiation, without special rites. The program of Sufism is very simple: To become saintly, you must remember God. That is all you have to do, but it is difficult task to achieve constantly. The Qur'an keeps repeating this centrality of *dhikr* over and over again: "Remember me and I remember you." So, you might say, then why go into all this meditation, chanting, and ritual? The problem is that the human mind is scattered. When we are sitting here and talking, you cannot concentrate on anything for more than a few moments and man in his fallen state is forgetful. We think of our lunch or meeting in the afternoon, and so on, but even things which are before our eyes we often do not remember! Much less do we remember the Divine Realities, which at the present moment seem absent from us.

So, all these Sufi techniques which some people do not understand and attack as *bid'ah* (innovation) are established to bring the mind together and enable us to remember God, to wake up from the state of negligence (*ghaflah*). Sufism contains the most profound and efficient methods of meditation, combined with invocation of the Names of

God often combined with chanting of poetry, music, and dancing, as we see in the Mawlawi Order.

Here I want to add the following remark: Sacred dancing in Sufism is important, because we are not only mind and soul but also body. Muslims believe that the body will be resurrected and that resurrection is both physical and spiritual. Muslims believe that the Prophet (peace be upon him) went on his *al-mi'raj* (nocturnal ascension) not only with his soul but also with his body. A spiritual ascension is possible for spiritual seekers. What is special in the ascension of the Prophet is that it was also physical. He ascended to the Divine Throne with his whole body.

EL-ZEIN: But you know that there is controversy on this issue. Some Muslim thinkers argue that the Prophet traveled by his soul, not by his body.

NASR: This is nonsense from the traditional point of veiw! Traditional Islam asserts that the Prophet ascended bodily (*al-mi'raj al-jismani*). It does not mean the same thing to say that only his soul ascended. A similar situation exists in Christianity, when we talk about Christ ascending to heaven bodily. Let us not forget that traditional Christianity believes that Christ was taken "bodily" to heaven! What ascended to heaven was not only the soul of Christ only, but the body of Christ as well! Traditional Catholics also believe that the Virgin Mary did not die. She was taken to Heaven "bodily." I have written extensively on this issue, and I am not going to expand more on it here!

But, to go back to this issue of Sufi dance which many people criticize, it is a sacred dance that integrates the body into one's inner being, which is in contact with the Divine Presence. If you watch people listening to a concert of serious classical music—for example, a concert of Bach's *St. Matthew's Passion*—you will see people sit still and listen to the music and appreciate it inwardly. But if you hear a concert of traditional Arab or Persian music, you will see that members of the audience listen but also move their bodies. The music is as spiritual as the music of Bach but the response is not only mental and emotional. You will see the same phenomenon if you go to India or Black Africa, because these civilizations have never become totally cerebral and cut off their spiritual contact with the body. In the modern West, people became to a large extent cerebral and the body came to be considered a machine. The result was that dancing in the West became a profane activity, mostly an activity to arouse sexual passions, while the Sufi dance is an esoteric dance meant to integrate soul, mind, and body.

EL-ZEIN: This integration of the body through dancing has also a cosmic dimension, since by whirling the dervishes imitate the circulating of the heavenly bodies.

NASR: Absolutely. But in the present-day context you have to be careful when using the terms "cosmos" and "cosmic." "Cosmos," in the modern sense, is nothing other than a mass of particles banging around, full of energy, with no meaning related to the world of the Spirit. Today it is becoming fashionable to speak about "cosmic consciousness, awareness," et cetera. But what do such terms really mean? What they should really mean is that there is a correspondence between us, as human beings, and the cosmos as seen traditionally. The cosmos as seen traditionally comprises the levels of reality below God, including the orders of the angels, which stand at higher levels of cosmic reality. The cosmos, in the Islamic sense, represents God's creation with all its multiple levels of reality, from the material to the spiritual, all that is below the Divine Order.

In that sense, yes, the Sufis accomplish a cosmic dance; they bring about a kind of *inshirah* (expansion) to "identify" with the cosmic reality. When we talk about the cosmos, we should mention the microcosm (*al-'alam al-saghir*) and the macrocosm (*al-'alam-al-kabir*). Both microcosm and macrocosm are reflections of the Metacosmic Reality.

When we talk about the integration of the Sufi with the cosmos, we should therefore be careful what we mean.

Integration is not scattering. What good is it for us to become integrated with all this Milky Way moving fast in space with its thousands of millions of particles of dust? It does not mean anything spiritually! Yes, the Milky Way reveals the grandeur of God's creation, but one cannot "identify" with it. What one can identify with is the spiritual reality of that divinely ordained order which in fact the word "cosmos" means traditionally, embracing all the levels of reality which are below God. But even they are steps toward the aim and preparation for reaching God.

Many people today, specifically those belonging to what is called New Age spirituality, talk about "Cosmic Consciousness." What can Cosmic Consciousness mean when the cosmos is understood in the modern scientific terms? One should really speak of "Metacosmic Consciousness." Cosmic Consciousness even if understood traditionally is a step toward the Metacosmic Consciousness.

Furthermore, some people do not need the step of cosmic consciousness to reach God. They go directly from the microcosm to God, like the great woman Sufi saint Rabi'ah al- 'Adawiyyah. There is a story told about her that on a beautiful spring day someone came to her and knocked at her door and said, "Come out and see how beautiful is God's creation: the trees and flowers are blooming." And Rabi'ah answered, "Why do not you come in and see how beautiful is God's garden within the soul?"

For some people, the association of nature with spiritual presence and, the appreciation of the cosmos as God's creation bearing His signs, is a very important step in their inner life, because they lead to the realization of the Divine and that is a very important dimension of authentic spirituality.

In any case, the Sufi practices to which you allude have as their ultimate function our integration through the spiritual path and means of reaching the Divine Reality. The awareness of our correspondences with the cosmos at large is a stage of the path. The way of union, *wisal*, includes always a stage of *inbisat, inshirah* (expansion) which precedes it. We have in fact the three supreme steps of the spiritual path: *qabd* (contraction), *bast* (expansion), and *wisal* (union), and *bast* includes a comic dimension.

In Islam, the cosmic identification to which you allude is in relation to the inner nature of the Prophet, to the Muhammadan Reality (*al-haqiqah al-Muhamadiyyah*), which means that the cosmic expansion of man is in relation to the Prophetic Substance, not to the Prophet as a man who lived in the seventh century in Arabia, not to his external reality, but to Muhammad as archetype of the whole of the cosmos as manifested by God. The deepest sense of *al-haqiqah al-Muhamadiyyah* is the inner reality of the cosmos and corresponds to the stage of *inbisat* in the stages of spiritual realization.

The Reality of Muhammad is closely connected to the theme of the Perfect Man. I have in mind specifically what 'Abd al-Karim al-Jili wrote in his *al-Insan al-kamil* and also to what Ibn 'Arabi himself wrote on this same issue.

EL-ZEIN: How can we define the Perfect Man?

NASR: This is the most important issue in Sufism after *wahdat al-wujud* (Oneness of Being or Unity of Reality). We can only define the Universal Man from on high, not from below; that is, in relation to God. The Universal Man is that being who reflects the totality of God's Names and Qualities. He is that being who is not limited by the governance of a single Divine Name but reflects all the Divine Names. He is a mirror in which God can contemplate Himself, as Ibn 'Arabi says. The Universal Man is the perfection of the human state as well as its prototype. You cannot define the Universal Man in terms of our ordinary imperfections and perfections. It is we who are defined by the Universal Man, we as men and women of this world. All the perfections we aspire to are due to the fact that the Universal Man exists at the center of our beings and is the inner reality of our beings. We are, in a sense, creatures who always live below the level of our full reality.

When the Qur'an says *thumma radadnahu asfala 'l-safilin* (Then do We abase him [to be] the lowest of the low), one of its meanings is precisely that we live below our level, because God created us in the best of stature *fi ahsan-i taqwim*, then He cast us into the world of time, of materiality, of imperfection.

Today, human beings are defined according to an external social norm or simply biologically. To be normal or abnormal is defined in accordance with what is considered to be normal externally in society. Sufism is just the other way round. In Sufism, a normal person is a saint, because the Universal Man is the norm in Sufism, and so we all live below the norm. In today's society a saint is abnormal, while a person who goes to work from nine to five, and who comes home and watches television, is considered to be the norm.

EL-ZEIN: You mentioned that the doctrine of the Perfect Man is the most important doctrine in Sufism after the Unity of Reality (*wahdat al-wujud*). You are one of the first who have written extensively in English on this theme, and one of its strongest adepts. What is *wahdat al-wujud*?

NASR: The Perfect or Universal Man is the full reflection of God's Names and Qualities and is at once the archetype of man and the cosmos. All human beings are potentially Universal Man, but that reality is actualized fully in only prophets and great saints. To understand this doctrine, we first have to comprehend the doctrine of *wahdat al-wujud*, which is not a doctrine that is meant to be understood in its deepest sense by everyone. One of the glories of the Islamic Revelation is that its doctrines are available for everyone, yet, at the same time, there are levels of meaning not all of which are for everyone.

To understand *wahdat al-wujud* is to understand *al-tawhid* (There is no god but God) at the highest level of the meaning of this expression. To understand it at the highest level requires one of two things: (1) a very high metaphysical understanding and intellectual intuition, which not everybody has; (2) an inner purification up to the stage where the soul experiences its own *fana'*, its own extinction, and thereby realizes *tawhid*. The understanding of *wahdat al-wujud* derives from these two sources: either an intellectual understanding that there can be only one Reality ultimately, intellectual being understood here, not in the modern sense of the term, as equivalent to rational, but in a gnostic sense, as in the Platonic intellect; or through inner experience which only those who have had it can bear witness. In that case, you have to trust those who claim to have had it.

Suhrawardi said once, "I am astounded that people trust the word of those who spend their time performing *rasd* (observation of the stars) and take their word for it, but they do not trust *rasd* of the astronomers of the stars of the spiritual world."

If you accept the word of those who have had the experience, you must accept the thesis that there is this miraculous possibility for the human being to experience his own nothingness, which is logically contradictory, for if we are nothing, we cannot experience it; we can have no consciousness of it. If we do, that is because *qalb al mu'min 'arsh al-rahman* (the heart of the believer is the throne of the Merciful); that is, God is within us and it is through that illuminated God knowledge that *wahdat al-wujud* is realized by man, because he is potentially the Universal Man and can also become so actually.

What has been said contains the deepest meaning of *ana 'l-haqq* (I am the Truth) of Hallaj. The ultimate *fana'* (annihilation) is when our ego dies and God says *ana* within us. The *ana 'l-haqq* of Hallaj is one of the earliest expressions in Sufism of *wahdat al-wujud* (Unity of Reality), though many people do not wish to talk about it or understand it in this way. The Hallajian formulation, moreover, deals with this truth from the pole of the subject rather than the object. What Hallaj wanted to say is that there is only one *ana*, only one "I," only the Supreme Subject. Only God can say "I," metaphysically speaking.

When a person reaches such a stage, he realizes that this table is not simply a table; this chair is not simply a chair. There is no reality independent of God, because God is *al-Haqq*. The word *al-haqq* in classical Arabic does not only mean Truth; it also means Reality. So, if we believe that the sky itself is an independent reality, we are a *mushrik* (a heretic). *Wahdat al-wujud* means that nothing has a reality unless it is God's Reality. It does not mean that this table is God. But it means that, to the extent that this table is real, its reality cannot be other than God. It means to realize that, in the words of Frithjof Schuon, "the world is plunged in God."

EL-ZEIN: Its reality is a *tajalli*, a reflection of the Reality of God?

NASR: Yes, *tajalliyat*, theophanies. Sufism has elaborated so much on this doctrine.

EL-ZEIN: In this sense, nature itself is a theophany; nature should be read as a theophany.

NASR: Yes.

EL-ZEIN: I want to go back to the cry of Hallaj: *ana 'l-haqq* (I am the Truth), and raise with you what has been labeled as the "Christian influence" on Islamic mysticism. In the book *Présence de Louis Massignon*, you wrote the following: "Hallaaj represents within Sufism the special grace of Christ as it manifests itself in the Islamic universe. He is a Christic Sufi, if we can use such a term, that is, he manifests *al-barakah al-'isawiyyah* as it is called in Arabic, within him. It is not that he was influenced by Christianity as another tradition, another religion. But the structure of Islam is such that, within the Islamic tradition there is a possibility of the shining forth of the rays of the founders of other religions, especially of Judaism and Christianity."[3] Can you elaborate, especially on the last sentence?

Nasr: Each religion has its own structure. Christianity is Christocentric, meaning that Christ is at the center of the religion, which is why no Christian will be angry if you call his religion Christianity, while a Muslim will be angry if you call his religion Muhammadism, because Islam is Theo centered, Allah centered, not Muhammad centered. Now, in this Christian universe, Christ is the sun (if we can apply this symbology). When the sun comes out during the day, all the stars disappear, for the rays of the sun eclipse the other stars. In Christianity, the prophets such as Moses, David, and Abraham are not forgotten, but they do not play an essential role in the spiritual and religious economy of the Christian universe. For example, you do not have in Christianity the prayer of Abraham with the same significance as you have in Islam.

El-Zein: You mean as in the end of the prayer, we say, "God, pray on our Prophet Muhammad as Thou prayed on our Prophet Abraham?"

Nasr: Right. But there are also other prayers. The Islamic universe is very different, precisely because it is the final synthesis of the religions that had gone before it. Islam might be compared to a night sky, where the Prophet is the full moon, while other stars also shine in the Muhammadan sky. It is not accidental that in Islam the moon is the symbol of the religion as we still see on the flag of many Muslim countries rather than the sun. In the Japanese flag, one can see the sun in the middle of the flag, while there is not a single Islamic flag with the sun standing by itself as the central symbol. Therein lies a very deep meaning: In spiritual astrology, the moon is the last of the planets which integrates all the cosmic influences from the heavens above it before these influences come to earth. The Prophet represents the moon in that aspect of its integrating function. In the night sky, the moon is the most evident and luminous of all lights. But other stars, which symbolize the other prophets, are also present. Islam itself is the whole sky. If we follow this symbol and understand the message it conveys, you can say that in Islam the Prophet is the central manifestation of God and so he leads us to God, for you cannot reach God as a Muslim without the help of the Prophet. This is of course an impossibility.

Nevertheless, God has allowed the other prophets, especially the prophets of the Abrahamic line, to manifest themselves within this Muhammadan universe (at this point I use this expression on purpose) as stars in the firmament, but not as a sun.

So, Christ is the central sun of the Christian universe, but it is not as the sun that he influences the Islamic world. Rather, he is a star in the Islamic firmament. Ibn 'Arabi elaborated in his *Fusus al-hikam* (Bezels of Wisdom) on this issue. He devoted a chapter to each prophet, to each form of wisdom in this work. Thus you have a *hikmah musawiyyah* (Mosaic wisdom), a *hikmah adamiyyah* (Adamic wisdom), and so forth, where each prophet is seen as a specific manifestation of the Logos.

Certain Sufis, called Christic Sufis, were not influenced by Christianity as a religion, or by Christian monks, but by the Christlike type of spirituality. They had a special love for Christ as he manifested himself in the Islamic universe. Other Sufis manifested their love for certain other prophets, such as David or Moses but always with the confines of the Islamic universe.

Ibn 'Arabi speaks at length of Christ in his *Futuhat*. He even calls Christ "my master" and had a particular inner relation with the Christic reality. He considers Christ to be the seal of Sanctity of the Abrahamic family, and Ibn 'Arabi considered himself to be the seal of Muhammadan sanctity, *al-wilayah al-muhamadiyyah*.

There are very elaborate and esoteric correspondences in Ibn 'Arabi's doctrine concerning this issue. The mistake that many orientalists make when they study those Sufis is that they think that, if someone is a Sufi who has a certain Christlike quality or attachment to Christ, he must be secretly a Christian or influenced by Christianity! This is not at all the case! It is God's will that the other prophets also perform a function in the Muhammadan universe, precisely because they are also elements of that religious universe.

EL-ZEIN: When you just mentioned the misinterpretations of the orientalists, were you alluding to Asín Palacios? Specifically, I have in mind his book *El-Islam Christianizado*.

NASR: That title means that the whole of Sufism is a manifestation of Christian influence within Islam. But I think also that, to a certain extent, what Asín was doing was to cover himself. He was a Catholic priest in the Spain of the 1920s and 1930s, in which hardly anyone dared to speak about the influence of Islam in Spain, including on such mystics as John of the Cross and Teresa of Avila, and the significance of the Islamic intellectual and spiritual worldview in that land! So when people attacked him as talking about this influence on Christian Spain, he would defend himself by saying, "Look, this Islamic influence is itself impregnated with Christianity!" But Asín Palacios was a great scholar. Look at all the positive studies he did on Islamic culture, and the influential works he wrote on Sufism in Andalusia! He produced the first major study of Ibn 'Arabi in a European language and wrote a major work on Dante and Islam. We must take these works into account.

Chapter 2

Sufism and Cosmology

EL-ZEIN: In your book *Introduction to Islamic Cosmological Doctrines*, you compare cosmology to traditional arts. You assert that both select from diverse forms to fit with the spirit of a particular tradition. Can you elucidate how cosmology and traditional arts are similar?

NASR: Let us take the traditional art of Islam, of Christianity, or of Hinduism: There were thousands of different forms, different symbols that could be used, but each of these arts took a particular set of forms, of symbols, of images through which it expressed its truths. For example, the Christians have, let us say, the form of the cathedral; the space is the shape of the body of Christ. They have the cross; they have the traditional art of iconography, of Christ, Mary, and various angels taken from the Christian universe as it can be seen in medieval cathedrals, like, let us say Notre-Dame or Chartres. Now there are thousands of other forms that could have been used; no traditional art can use every form. That is not a possibility, but each traditional art chooses certain figures and symbols from the multiplicity of forms and symbols available to it, as has Hindu art, as has Islamic art, to create a traditional art which then speaks the language of that religion, of that religious universe to which the art belongs. In medieval cathedrals you experience the Christian universe; every element speaks as a symbol of that universe. But it does not include every form of symbolism on the surface of the earth. It does not include symbols which are used in Japanese art or Hindu art or Islamic art, even if there are certain symbols such as the sun or tree that are present in more than one traditional art.

Now cosmologies in a sense are the same way. In each tradition there is not only one cosmology. Even within a single traditional universe, like the Islamic one, there can be several cosmologies, all of which are ways of depicting the universe in such a way as to reveal the spiritual significance of the universe as seen by the particular religion in question. For example, Islam is based on the doctrine of unity, *tawhid*. All the different traditional cosmologies that are depicted in Islamic civilization by the philosophers or by the Sufis are rooted on the Qur'an and the *Hadith*. There are many different cosmologies and they are not the same in details, but they all point to the One. They are all ways of relating the world of multiplicity to the one single Divine Principle. Cosmologies are like traditional art in the sense of dealing with the multiplicity of phenomena, but always in relation to the One Divine Reality.

Let me add that we should not be fooled with thinking that modern science is "*the* science of the world of nature." It is *a* science that is not based on the Divine Principle, but on empiricism and rationalism, on a secular worldview. That is how it differs from traditional cosmologies. But Islamic cosmology, like Christian cosmology, Hindu cosmology, or Buddhist cosmology, is like the traditional arts of these great religions in the sense that they cannot exhaust all the different possible schemas but reveal, nevertheless, the patterns of the structure of the cosmos, its inner structures relating to fundamental principles, which for Islam is above all Divine Unity.

EL-ZEIN: You often seem to emphasize that cosmology involves the observer and is not a science independent from him like mathematics or pure physics. What role does the observer have while studying cosmology?

NASR: Even mathematics and physics are not completely independent from the subject who discovers them and knows them. The subject or the knower who studies the cosmos looks at it from a particular perspective, obviously, which affects his knowledge of it, one might say. This truth is evident especially in traditional cosmologies. If you are a Muslim, your mind is determined by the Islamic Revelation. And if you are a Christian, you will be influenced by the Christian Revelation, and so on and so forth. And so a particular revelation affects the thinker who writes about these cosmologies. The truth is even subtler than that. The traditional universe itself, the sector of the cosmos where a particular revelation or religion is revealed, in a sense is transformed by that revelation. For example, Muslims look at the first moon of Ramadan in a particular way, whereas a Christian will only find in it to be a crescent moon. For him the moon is related to waning and waxing. So this part of the cosmos is Islamized for Muslims.

EL-ZEIN: In your study of cosmology, you mention the "Greater Mysteries" and the "Lesser Mysteries." How do you define them?

NASR: I use these terms because it was well known in the classical West as well as in the Middle Ages when a distinction was made between the Greater Mysteries and the Lesser Mysteries. The first Mysteries refer to the Nature of God, to the highest metaphysical truths. But the Lesser Mysteries deal with the nature of the cosmos, of the world and also with the microcosm, which is our soul, all in relation to the Greater Mysteries. But here, of course, the word "mystery" also means the hidden, the esoteric, and the inner, not just external sciences in themselves. The external science of modern astronomy is not a lesser mystery. It is not a mystery at all. Modern science does not believe in mystery in the traditional sense; rather it tries to remove mystery by supposedly knowing it scientifically.

So I am using this term to refer to the cosmological sciences as the Lesser Mysteries in comparison with the science of the Divine Principle Itself. The Lesser Mysteries concern the science of the manifestation of the Divine Principle, the science of the creation of the world in relation to its Creator. It is the knowledge of creation in light of the knowledge of the Creator, of God, not of creation irrespective of God, which is not a Lesser Mystery at all. Traditional cosmology is always a knowledge of the cosmos, but in light of the Divine Principle, as going back to the Principle and reflecting the wisdom of the Divine Principle. And so, there is a distinction to be made in the Western esoteric tradition, which between the two Mysteries is very pertinent.

EL-ZEIN: You have mentioned Islamic cosmology, Hindu cosmology, Christian cosmology, et cetera. What does that mean? Are we not talking about one universe that should have one cosmology?

NASR: In the highest sense, yes, and in the deeper sense of the inner meaning of the universe, yes. But since we live in the world of multiplicity, and God has allowed different segments of humanity to exist, and He has allowed different religions to exist, different perspectives to exist, and also different aptitudes and attitudes, different ways of looking at things, but all in light of the One Truth. The richness of God's creativity would not allow only one cosmology to exist. Let me give you an example since you are yourself a poet and a writer: Ideally, there should be only one language, the *Ursprach* about which Germans speak, the "divine language," and the source of all languages. But because of the multiplicity of the recipients that belong to different phases of human history, because of races and ethnic groups, we have a multiplicity also of revelations and languages.

So, yes, there is one single cosmology in the deeper sense based on the realization that the whole Universe comes from God, that there is one language, ideally, which is the language of our relationship with God, the language of silence that we all share. But as soon as you want to speak, as soon as you come out of silence, you have to speak in a particular language, and, therefore, you have the multiplicity of languages as you have the multiplicity of traditional cosmologies, which does not negate what you are talking about, which is the inner unity of all these cosmologies, that they always reflect the single Divine Wisdom, the one Divine Reality. That is why both Titus Burkhardt and myself have spoken of *Cosmologia Perennis* like you have *Philosophia Perennis*. There are many traditional philosophies, Islamic, Chinese, Platonic, Hindu, Taoist, et cetera. They are all authentic expressions of the *Philosophia Perennis*. In the same way, there are various cosmologies that can be said to be different versions of one single *Cosmologia Perennis*.

El-Zein: Maybe the Gnostics through their mystical experiences can grasp that different cosmological expressions are different expressions of the *Cosmologia Perennis*. I am particularly thinking here of Ibn 'Arabi.

Nasr: Exactly. Definitely, Ibn 'Arabi, the great master, who had the supreme Spiritual experience, who had a great knowledge of God, *al-shaykh al-akbar, al 'arif bi'Llah*, described the Universe in more than one manner. He had the experience of "seeing" the whole universe as the Self-disclosure of God. There is a wonderful book written by my former student and friend William Chittick entitled precisely *The Self-Disclosure of God*. It is a remarkably well-done work on Ibn 'Arabi's cosmology which shows that all the cosmologies described by him are depiction of God's Self-disclosure, so that we can say that God is Self-disclosing Himself in His creation and there are different ways Ibn 'Arabi describes that self-disclosure in more than one language. The experiences that Ibn 'Arabi and Lao

Tzu, for example, had of the supreme meaning of nature, of the cosmos as the disclosure of Divine Reality, point to the truth and testify to the fact that there cannot be but one Universe and one supreme knowledge of it even if that knowledge is expressed in different languages. But the sciences, which described this supreme experience of the Self-disclosure of God, often did so by expressing different aspects of this Self-disclosure. There must be more than one science of the cosmos, precisely because it is the cosmos. If God is one, His Creation is many. Therefore, there is a multiplicity of ways of knowing and describing those *tajalliyat* or theophanies that God enables us to know.

After spending half a century studying Islamic cosmologies, I have come to realize more and more the different shades of meaning in various cosmologies, how precious each one is and how they all point to the same ultimate Reality. Again, coming back to the comparison with Islamic art, on the one hand we have one Islamic art; on the other hand, we have such different expressions of this art. Mamluk art is not identical with Safavid art, which is not identical with Andalusian art, but they are all Islamic art and reflect shades of the beauty, meaning, and creativity of Islamic art. All are extremely precious. If you eliminated any of these schools, you would lose a great richness, as they are all notable peaks of Islamic art. We can also evoke Maghribi art, Ottoman art, Seljuk art, all of which reveal the remarkable creativity of Islamic art. Moreover, they all belong to the same universe of meaning and reveal many of the same symbols.

When you are inside the Sultan Ahmad Mosque in Istanbul or in Ibn Tulun Mosque in Cairo, or in the Corodoba Mosque, not all the forms are the same, but you are in the same formal and spiritual ambiance. Now, transpose that reality to the world of cosmology and you will see what I mean. Cosmology is not meant for everyone. It is meant for those who can study it, but it underlies Islamic art and architecture, which all Muslims can experience. There is no traditional and sacred architecture without cosmology; and this truth holds in every civilization. The reason why the modern world in general cannot produce a sacred architecture is that it has lost its cosmology in the sense we understand it, in the traditional sense of the word.

Like the different forms of Islamic arts, we have different Islamic cosmological schemes. I described some of them in my book *Introduction to Islamic Cosmological Doctrines*, where I studied Ikhwan al-Safa, al-Biruni, and Ibn Sina. Because human types are not identical, a great tradition, which is still alive, has to be able to have within itself the possibility of catering to the needs of different human types. If it does not, it becomes like what happened to European Christianity toward the end of the Middle Ages. Some people stayed in the Church; others left. We see this phenomenon especially during the Renaissance. Not everyone was able to find what he was looking for within the existing Christian intellectual universe, and that situation caused breaches in Western Christianity.

Such an event did not happen in Islam at that time because Islam was always able to provide for the intellectual and spiritual needs of different human types within *Dar al-Islam*. There were some people who were attracted by, let us say, a kind of illuminationist cosmology, like that of Suhrawardi, based on the symbolism of light and different levels of illumination. Others were drawn to ontology and the language of being and levels of existence going back to Ibn Sina and culminating in Mulla Sadra, with his philosophy of *wujud* with its *ta'ayyunat* and *tajalliyat*. Others were attached to the theosophy of Ibn 'Arabi and the many versions that developed after him. Others were drawn to very simple, poetic versions of these cosmologies, which we have both in Arabic and in Persian without elaborate philosophical underpinnings, like the poem of the Burda and the beautiful *al-Salat al-mashishiyyah* (prayer on the Prophet

Muhammad) of Ibn Mashish. These poems are actually cosmological, because they deal with the cosmic aspects of the Muhammadan Reality. So, Islam was able to provide these different types of cosmologies for different types of human beings. This is a very fascinating and remarkable field to which not much attention has been paid until now in contemporary scholarship.

EL-ZEIN: Why do you think Islam was capable of offering these different types? Is it due to the fact that Islam is a religion of synthesis? We know for example that Ikhwan al-Safa' incorporated Pythagorean thought, others Platonism, not to mention the notion of cosmic cycles taken from Hinduism, et cetera.

NASR: Yes. There are two elements in Islam, which are related together as far as this question of yours is concerned. The first one is that Islam is the last religion, the last major revelation of this cycle of human history, and history bears witness to this truth. No major religion has come after it, and the Prophet Muhammad is considered by us as the "Seal of the Prophets." There have been small manifestations of new religious movements, such as Sikhism, born of the encounter of two major traditions, Hinduism and Islam, but there has not been a major religion, like Christianity or Buddhism, coming after Islam.

Now the finality of Islam is related to this synthesis that this religion has always had. Islam was given by God tremendous synthetic power because its function, providential function, was to synthesize the essence of the revelatory truths that went before it. And Islam had an easier task of integrating ideas from the pre-Islamic civilizations and religions than Christianity did, which also absorbed much of Greco-Roman thought. So, this is one element of the two I mentioned.

The second element is the emphasis of Islam upon *tawhid* (Oneness or Unity); by its nature, since it was revealed to unveil the Highest Principle and to synthesize all that flows from It. If a religion concentrates, let us say, on a particular messenger, as does Christianity on Christ, it is more difficult to absorb and integrate into its perspective truths of another religion. That is why Christians have more trouble coming to terms with Islam than Islam has when coming to terms with Christianity. But if one concentrates on the Supreme Reality, which for us is Allah, the One, who is above every determination, then what "flows" from the One is much easier to integrate within that perspective. These are very subtle, metaphysical qualities of the Islamic revelation, but on the actual level of history you can see that they enabled the Muslims to integrate into their worldview so much that had existed before Islam. That is why Arabic, which was used as the first and only important philosophical and scientific language of Islam, before Persian came into play, is one of the richest languages in the world. A lot of scientific and philosophical texts in Arabic are of Greek origin, many of which do not exist in Greek, and the same is true of Syriac, Pahlavi, and Sanskrit. It is unbelievable how such Arabic literature is not only for Islam but also for many other traditions. But the main thrust of the creative energy of Islamic society supported this extensive movement of translation which made Arabic a major source for works pertaining to pre-Islamic civilizations.

EL-ZEIN: In your book *Introduction to Islamic Cosmological Doctrines*, you strongly link cosmology to angelology. Why is the angel given this tremendous role in Sufism. And in a way is it not contradictory to what God says about the angels in the Qur'an, where they are less knowledgeable than man, to whom God has taught the names of all things?

NASR: It is in *Surat al-Baqarah* (chapter of the Cow) where it is mentioned that God taught Adam the names. But no, the various roles given to the angels in the Qur'an is not in contradiction to the above Qur'anic teaching, which in fact emphasizes the role of angels on all levels of cosmic existence, not to mention the *Hadith*. There are hundreds of *Hadiths* about the role of angels in the cosmos and in human life nearby, because God does not always act directly in this world but does so mostly through angelic agencies. We believe that everything that takes place in the world of nature is done through God's Will mostly through His agents; and the angels are His agents.

From one point of view, man is below the rank of angels. In Islamic cosmology, oftentimes you see mention of God in His transcendent Reality above the whole of the cosmos, and then the archangelic world, then the angelic world, then the world of jinn and men, then the world of animals, and then the world of plants and minerals. There is the great hierarchy of existence in which angels stand above man in his terrestrial state. From another point of view, however, man can go beyond the angels, because the angels have a fixed position in the hierarchy of existence, whereas man can journey through all of the levels of existence and go even beyond the angels to reach God Himself. That is why man can know certain things which the angels cannot know. Here is where Satan made his great mistake; that is, he mistook his position in the hierarchy of being as an angel with the creature whom God created from clay and dust, from the earth, but into whom He breathed His own Spirit. And that means that man has the capability of going beyond the angelic world to reach the Divine Abode itself and attain the Supreme knowledge of God Himself. Therein lies the superiority of man. As far as the cosmic hierarchy is concerned, however, man stands below the level of angels. We human beings can try to emulate the angels and possess angelic qualities, because angelic reality is within us but above our ordinary consciousness.

EL-ZEIN: To reach the angelic realm, Sufis often speak of going on a voyage. Why the voyage? Why do we need to reach the angelic world through a voyage?

NASR: It is very simple. The reason there is a voyage, a symbolism of voyage, a wayfaring, a *sayr*, is that God is there and we are here metaphysically, we are already "in God," *fi 'Llah*, but to actually reach Him requires a voyage, a *sayr ila 'Llah* and ultimately *fi'Llah* which in most cases requires journeying through the angelic realms.

We are in the human state, and the goal of Sufism is to enable us to reach our *fitrah*, the state in which God created us in perfection when we were in the Divine Proximity and before our fall. But since we have fallen from that state, we have to go back from where we are to where we should be, that is, His *qurb*, or proximity, and this process requires a spiritual journey. Now is it necessary to go through all the levels of the cosmos in order to reach the end of the journey? These are good questions. Is cosmology necessary for spirituality? My response is no, not necessary in all cases. There are certain people who are permitted and guided by God to make a direct flight not having to go through the various levels and layers of the cosmos. Their inner structure is such that they can soar, sort of directly from the human state to God, like Rabi'ah al-'Adawiyyah. She is a very good example of that possibility. Rumi speaks about this matter in a beautiful poem. He states that there is a relation without "howness" and without analogy between the Lord of the soul, that is God, and the soul of man. And because of the direct nexus that we have with God, it is possible for certain types of human beings to travel directly to God and not to be concerned with the cosmos. That is why certain types of Sufis did not write about cosmology. But that is not the whole story.

Certain other people are created in such a way that they have to journey through all the levels of cosmic reality to reach the Metacosmic Reality, because man has also a cosmic dimension. No complete spirituality in any tradition could be devoid of this dimension. That is where all complete spiritualities, that is, Islamic, Christian, Jewish, Hindu, and Buddhist (in its Vajrayana and Mahayana forms) also have a cosmology. So, spiritualization is also related to cosmology in the journey to the Beyond.

It is interesting that the prototype of all spiritual Realization in Islam is the *mi'raj* (ascension) of the Prophet where he goes through all the levels of the cosmos, at the end of which he approaches the *qaba qawsayn aw adna* (he was two bows' lengths away or even closer), which is the highest station that is even beyond the archangelic realm. That is why Gabriel did not accompany him in this last stage. The *mi'raj* is the perfect model of journeys through the cosmos.

EL-ZEIN: That is, perhaps, why we have many Sufis imitating the Prophet's *mi'raj*; for example, Bayazid Bastami who wrote his own *mi'raj*.

NASR: Of course. Not only did they write about the *mi'raj*, but they also experienced it. Some Sufis have written about it, some have not. But it remains a central experience. We have the famous Hadith *al-salat mi'raj al-mu'min* (the canonical prayer is the ascension of the believer). Even the daily prayers for the real faithful should be a *mi'raj*, a *'uruj*, an ascension of the spirit to God. The difference, however, between the Prophet's *mi'raj* and the Sufi's *mi'raj* is that the latter can never achieve the bodily *mi'raj* which the Prophet accomplished and which is a miracle that God wanted him to perform. This is metaphysically very significant, because his *mi'raj* integrated all the levels of human existence, which includes the bodily, and, in a sense, it is like resurrection in which our body participates, not only our soul. In this world, however, other human beings can only experience the spiritual *mi'raj*. Nevertheless, the experience of the *mi'raj* is essential in Sufism, and it shows the relationship between religious cosmology and the prototype of spiritualization.

EL-ZEIN: So, we have then two kinds of Sufi writings; one experiential and one contemplative, composed by Sufis who belonged to the *ishraqi* philosophy and who wrote a lot about the spiritual voyage. The first one is epitomized by Rabi'ah al-'Adawiyyah, who once had a friend knocking at her door and saying to her, "It is so beautiful outside, why don't you go out?" and she responded, I think . . .

NASR: Yes, she said, "Why don't you come in and see how much more beautiful it is inside?" which is a certain possibility that some Sufis have manifested, as I mentioned before. The other school, which we talked about as metaphysical description of wayfaring, is not confined to those who were attracted by *ishraqi* philosophy. It includes, in fact, almost all other forms of Sufi "philosophy." Ibn 'Arabi's Sufi metaphysics, for example, was not influenced directly by *ishraqi* philosophy, and he wrote very extensively about wayfaring, about what we could term as "esoteric cosmology" as well as of course metaphysics itself.

EL-ZEIN: His metaphysics and cosmology could be summarized into five *hadraat*.

NASR: That is right. He had a very profound metaphysical view of the cosmos, which he considered as self-manifestation of God. And Ibn 'Arabi used the expression *hadrah* in its technical Sufi sense, which means presence. He also used the expression *wahdat al-wujud* (Unity of Being), which became common in Sufism. These doctrines are intellectual and both refer to the basic "structure," one might say, of reality.

EL-ZEIN: It is essentially consciousness, right?

NASR: In a sense, yes, *Wujud* is being, existence, and consciousness all together, while in the English language existence could refer to simply a dead creature out there without consciousness.

Ibn 'Arabi talks about the five *hadraat* that you have mentioned, and he does so in the context of the traditional chain of being. These five *hadraat* are, first, the *hahut*, which is the Essence of the Divine. Then comes *lahut*, which refers to the Names and Qualities of God. *Lahut* and *hahut* together comprise the Divine Reality. In the Qur'an, Allah is shown to have an Essence, as well as Names and Qualities. Then we have the *jabarut*, the *malakut*, and, finally, the *mulk*. Therefore, respectively to archangelic, angelic, and physical worlds. *Mulk* is sometimes used to refer to the terrestrial world in which man lives.

EL-ZEIN: Concerning the term *lahut*, it is less and less used in the contemporary Muslim world. It is even becoming in some countries of the Arab world a "heretical" word, essentially referring to Christian theology!

NASR: But the reason why is the other way round; that is, since Christian Arabs use it all the time to describe a Christian theological idea, it has gained a Christian theological connotation. Hence, Muslim Arabs in general do not use it often, while it is often used by Arab Sufis. It is also used regularly in Persian, Turkish, Urdu, and other languages where this problem did not come up. Although there are some Christian Persians, they are not as many of them as there are in Lebanon and Syria.

Anyway, below *lahut*, you have the world of *jabarut*, which is the world of pure "divine determination," *al-jabr*. It is the higher angelic world, while the world below it, *malakut*, is the realm of the lower angelic world; it is the world immediately above the physical and terrestrial world. It is also in a certain sense the imaginal world, *'alam al-khayal*, the world of not human but cosmic imagination to which Suhrawardi and Mulla Sadra refer. Then you have *'alam al-mulk*, which is the physical world understood traditionally. So, in this manner a profound cosmology was developed, which showed that all these levels are really levels of the presence of the Divine Reality, of God's Names and Qualities, but in different manifestations the totality of which comprises the whole of the cosmos. There is, of course, another way to explain the doctrine of *wahdat al-wujud*, and that is to point to the inner meaning of the *shahada la ilaha illa 'Llah* (there is no god but God) itself.

EL-ZEIN: Since you mentioned the imaginal world, how do you view the role of imagination in Islamic cosmology, and in particular how would you define the *barzakh*?

NASR: This is a very large question. It is treated differently by different traditional authors. First of all, the *barzakh* is in the Qur'an itself. It is the intermediary state, between Hell and Paradise. Its various inner levels of meaning are not developed extensively by the early Sufis and Islamic philosophers, but rather by Suhrawardi and Ibn 'Arabi. They developed a very elaborate doctrine of the imaginal. It is interesting that this esoteric doctrine of the imaginal world is missing in the Western cosmology and traditional Christian cosmology. But now it is being revived, and many in the West talk about it, such as the French writer Gilbert Durand. But it is especially Henry Corbin who explained fully the doctrine of the imagination to the Western world when he wrote his famous book *L'imagination créatrice dans le soufisme d'Ibn 'Arabi*. Corbin also coined the term "imaginal" to distinguish this term, as it should be understood, from imaginary, which has come to mean unreal in everyday French or English.

EL-ZEIN: You mentioned Suhrawardi and Ibn 'Arabi, who treated the theme of imagination in Sufism. How about Islamic philosophers, how did they deal with imagination? I have particularly in mind the great Ibn Sina.

NASR: I was going to talk precisely about Ibn Sina. In Islamic philosophy, when we talk about the imagination, we need to go back to him. So much goes back to Ibn Sina. He wrote about *'alam al-khayal*, but in its macrocosmic aspect, drawing from Aristotelian sources but interpreting it in a different way and elaborating on it. Ibn Sina showed that the imagination plays a role as a faculty with a cognitive aspect. Later on, Suhrawardi and Ibn 'Arabi explored further the idea and reality and established a whole cosmology of *'alam al-khayal*. Suhrawardi was the first to say that *'alam al-khayal* is not only in the individual mind, you might say, to use a modern terminology but that there was also a cosmic *'alam al-khayal*. Ibn 'Arabi expounded this thesis and took it even further all the way to the Divine Reality, and to the creative power of God. For Ibn 'Arabi, *'alam al-khayal* is within ourselves and is also the manifestation of the Divine Reality in the cosmos and, you might say, reaching its highest level. You can right now imagine a pink cow or a two-headed bull. Your imagination can create an indefinite number of forms. You do not think; thinking has to do with concepts, which is another part of the mind, but you can also imagine forms. Ibn 'Arabi says that this power or reality is not just fantasy but has in fact a reality that corresponds to cosmic reality. The difference is that we cannot existentiate what we imagine. Only God can, or certain prophets and saints given that power by Him.

Now, later on, this doctrine was much further elaborated by Mulla Sadra, the great master of the metaphysics of *'alam al-khayal*. In Western cosmology, even in medieval times, you had only the physical world, the angelic world, and the Divine world. In traditional Islamic cosmology the world immediately above the physical world is the imaginal world in which, as Muslim authorities have said, the forms are without matter, that would resemble the matter we find in our physical and visible world. They also call the imaginal world *'alam al suwar al mu'allqah*, the "world of hanging forms," that is, forms without matter. In both the imaginal and the purely intelligible world we have already transcended the world of forms. The fact that in certain cosmologies, we also have subtle matter and levels of matter is another question into which I shall not go here. Anyway, this fully developed philosophy of the imaginal world led later on to the development of a very rich Islamic philosophy, epistemology, and eschatology which raised questions of the kind, Where will some events of the Judgment Day take place? They can be neither in the physical world nor in the purely intelligible world, because the latter does not participate in change. Such events were said by later Islamic thinkers to belong to the imaginal world. When we die, we go to this imaginal world, which is composed of several *barazikh*. There is not only one *barzakh*.

There are many of them because you have levels of the imaginal world. You have higher *barazikh*, which are paradisiacal, and lower ones, which are infernal. It is into this imaginal world, more real than this world, which we experience here below, that we shall go when we die.

El-Zein: I know this session is devoted to cosmology, but since we are talking about the imagination and the imaginal world and since the philosophy of art is related to the philosophy of the imagination, I would like to divert the discussion for a little to art. How do you relate this imaginal world to art?

Nasr: Good question. In the West, imagination is considered to be only in the mind of the artist. It does not have any objective correspondence to the cosmic imaginal world, to any existential reality. It is derived from the human mind and that is one of the reasons why modern art is so subjective. It is hard to understand what is going on, whereas in traditional art the imagination of the artist in a sense draws from the cosmic imagination and the archetypes of the visible reality, from the Platonic ideas which are also reflected in the imaginal world. In this way, traditional art creates forms that then become available in the physical realm.

El-Zein: All this discussion on the role of the imagination and the imaginal raises a question: Can we human beings evolve on the path to spirituality without imagination?

Nasr: This is a possibility in certain cases, but usually spirituality involves sensitivity to and awareness of the imaginal world. Great spiritual figures, and especially Sufi masters, have had this sensitivity and also intimate knowledge of this intermediate world. We see that reality in the

Christian tradition as well. In Islam, not all the Sufis wrote or spoke much of the imaginal world, but most of them did so in one way or another. And that is also a reason why in Islam the spiritual life has contributed to artistic creativity, to the vast outpouring of poetry, of calligraphy, of miniatures, of music, of architecture, et cetera. Almost all creations of Islamic art come essentially from people who have had access to the higher level of the imaginal world. We should not forget the fact that the imaginal world has also a lower level, which contains demonic forms, negative forms. The imaginal world opens to us both its paradisiacal and demonic domains, in addition to what concerns out ordinary life here on earth.

EL-ZEIN: Since the imaginal domain is just above our physical realm, does that mean that we are surrounded by it?

NASR: That is right, definitely. But in modern times we do not usually concern ourselves with the cosmic dimension of the imaginal world but only with the imaginal world that is within our psyche.

EL-ZEIN: The *jinn* inhabit this intermediary, imaginal world. How do you define them?

NASR: The jinn are psychic beings having consciousness like men. Some verses of the Qur'an refer to the *jinn* and men together.

EL-ZEIN: What do you mean exactly? Do they not exist out there?

NASR: Of course they do as an order within creation distinct from man but in contact with him. In the modern perspective, people associate the psyche only with a living person. We do not accord any macrocosmic reality to the world of the psyche, whereas in traditional Islamic cosmology, as you know, even the stars, the planets, and the celestial spheres have their own *nafs*, their own soul or *'aql*, and there is also universal soul, *al nafs al-kulliyyah*. The *jinn* belong to this psychological world between the corporeal and the intelligible. They do not have physical bodies like us but *can* appear also in corporeal forms.

Now, we can be aware of this psychological world in its cosmic aspect because we also contain the various levels of reality within ourselves and also have been given by God the possibility of knowing the levels of reality both microcosmic and macrocosmic. The psychological world is open, on the one hand, vertically, to the divine world and, on the other hand, down below to the physical world. Now *jinn* are like us in the sense they are created by God, they have awareness, they have a "mind," being psychic realities, but they do not have physical bodies. You cannot be a Muslim, at least not a traditional one, without believing in the reality of the *jinn*. But also you cannot subjectivize the *jinn* because of a sense of inferiority complex vis-à-vis the modern world and the modern scientific point of view. Modern science would tell you that belief in the *jinn* is superstition or a subjective state, because scientists cannot observe the *jinn* scientifically, measure them, study their activities, et cetera. The *jinn* belong to what is called "subtle manifestation," which is not quantifiable and measurable through modern scientific means.

EL-ZEIN: I want to come back to the hierarchy within the cosmos, to this view of the cosmos organized in five *hadraat*, as Ibn 'Arabi says, and as we have just discussed. You have said somewhere that to understand Islamic cosmology you have to use the language of symbols. Are you advocating that we should be interpreters and decoders of symbols?

NASR: Like all traditional writers, I use the term symbol as having an ontological reality. The symbol is not man-made. It relates a lower mode of existence to a higher mode of existence. If we do not understand the language of symbolism, how are we going to move from a lower level of reality to a higher one? For example, we look at the world, and we try to understand it literally. What happens? We end up with modern astronomy and physics, which has a special literal interpretation of the world. But if you understand the world symbolically, the visible world, *'alam al-shahadah*, is seen to symbolize the invisible world, *'alam al-ghayb*, otherwise you cannot even speak of *'alam al-ghayb* meaningfully. But the symbols lead us to that world. That is why I made the statement to which you refer in your question. That is why also in all religions, cosmology is couched in symbolic language. Even its mathematical aspect has a symbolic dimension. Now, it is, of course, possible to develop a philosophical and metaphysical language to express cosmology, but it is always in a sense an explication and interpretation of an already existing symbolic cosmology. The Qur'an, for example, speaks of the cosmos not in its external aspect alone but symbolically even of the external aspect being a symbolic expression of a higher reality. In the *ayat al nur* (the Light Verse), we have the olive tree, the lamp, light upon light, the East and the West. Each word in this verse is a symbol.

Every religion provides several cosmologies. Like several forms of traditional art, there are several traditional cosmologies. For example, the Islamic art of the Maghrib is different from the Persian one, but both are Islamic art. Cosmology is in a sense a sacred art. In Hinduism we have different cosmological schemes, and Islam has different ones as well. You have in Islamic cosmology Avicenian cosmology, that of the the Ikhwan al-Safa', that of Ibn 'Arabi and later on of Mulla Sadra. You have the school of Central Asia represented by Najm al-Din Kubra with its symbolism of light. All these cosmological schemes are very elaborate expressions of Islamic cosmological doctrines. Even within the works of Ibn 'Arabi, within one single author, one can find different cosmological schemes; for example, the cosmology based on the letters of the alphabet and the astrological scheme of cosmology. Titus Burckhardt wrote a wonderful book, a brilliant book on Ibn 'Arabi's astrology as he depicted it in *al-Futuhat al-Makkiyyah*.

EL-ZEIN: Since you mentioned Ibn 'Arabi and his cosmological works, I am thinking of Suhrawardi, who also spoke of different mountains bearing different letters of the Arabic alphabet. He talks, for example, of the mountain *Sad*, the mountain *Nun*, the mountain *Qaf*. What does that mean with regard to Islamic cosmology?

NASR: This is a very good question. First of all, in the Islamic cosmos, the cosmic mountain is identified as Mt. Qaf, whose name is the same as the letter *Qaf* of the Arabic alphabet. It is interesting that the Qur'an has a chapter called *Qaf*, which is associated with the letter *Qaf* in which there is a reference to cosmology. Now, when Suhrawardi speaks about these mountains bearing names of letters, he is speaking about various levels of reality, and he does so in a very elaborate manner.

EL-ZEIN: You speak too about the cosmic mountain in your books. You also mention the two "cities" or climes of *Jabulqa* and *Jabulsa*, and you make a comparison between them and the Holy Mountain of the Grail. Can you elaborate on this?

NASR: First of all, the two "cities" of *Jabulqa* and *Jabulsa* are two cities that belong to the eighth clime. You have seven classical climes in this world. The eighth clime is the world immediately transcending our physical world, and it corresponds to *'alam al-khayal*. The stories concerning these two "cities" are symbolic and there is a profound symbolism related to them. However, this does not mean they are unreal. On the contrary they are very real in Islamic sacred geography.

Now, these cities have their own geography and topography, but they belong to the imaginal world. The story of the Grail is also a mythical story in which the heroes are in quest of the Holy Grail hidden at the foot of the Sacred

Mountain. This is not a physical mountain, but a mountain that belongs to the symbolic topography of that world.

EL-ZEIN: You are alluding here to sacred geography. How does it relate to cosmology?

NASR: Sacred geography is one component in cosmology, while cosmology is the science of the whole of reality and of all levels of existence below the Divine Order. Sacred geography is a very important traditional science. It is the science of sacred spaces, sacred loci, sacred topographies of the earth, sacred features of our earth and other "earths." We usually think of one earth that we contrast to Heaven. But there is more than one earth. In the Qur'an there are allusions to them. Ibn 'Arabi talks about this matter in his *Futuhat*. And Corbin has also dealt extensively with this subject.

Some of the Ishraqi (Illuminationist) philosophers developed a very elaborate cosmology based on these multiple "earths." This notion is not totally absent from modern cosmology in the West, although here the vertical dimension is missing. We have, for example, in modern Western cosmology parallel worlds, which are not parallel in the sense that one universe is here and another next to it and above it, but they are parallel in the sense they represent totally different universes. Sometimes, ideas in modern Western cosmology echo some traditional ideas, but without the metaphysical depth.

EL-ZEIN: Since you mentioned Islamic and Western cosmology, I would like to tie this topic to two different approaches to the cosmos in two different works. The first one is entitled *Hayy Ibn Yaqzan*, written by a Muslim philosopher, Ibn Tufayl, and also before him by another Muslim philosopher and mystic, Ibn Sina; and another book, which is not about cosmology per se, *Robinson Crusoe*, written by a British author, Daniel Defoe, in the seventeenth century. In the first work, the hero, *Hayy Ibn Yaqzan*, grew up on an island completely isolated from the rest of humanity.

Robinson Crusoe is a novel that was first published in 1719, and is sometimes considered to be the first novel in English. It is also likely that Defoe was inspired by the Latin or English translations of Ibn Tufayl's *Hayy Ibn Yaqzan*.

Although Defoe expresses some Puritan Protestant ethics and praises, the book is not so much interested in metaphysics as it is in cultural relativism and in his own survival. Crusoe invents tools and builds a home, while Hayy of Ibn Tufayl is turned toward the knowledge of the Divine. How do you view the difference between Islamic cosmology and Western cosmology through these two works?

Nasr: *Hayy Ibn Yaqzan* of Ibn Tufayl is a very profound work that has often been misunderstood by many modern Arab scholars who stressed the aspect of "naturalism" about it. There is, however, nothing naturalistic in it in the ordinary sense of the word, although Hayy lives alone on an island and without any contact with humanity and arrives to the knowledge of God. And when a person brought up in an ordinary civilization that has knowledge of the Revelation comes from a nearby island, Hayy has already knowledge of the Revelation. This does not mean that Revelation is not necessary; it is rather a confirmation of the revelatory aspect of the intellect within us. Metaphysically speaking, the Prophet (PBUH) is the last cosmic objective manifestation of a reality which exists on a smaller scale within the human being when the intellect or *'aql*, is functioning within him. In a sense, *'aql* in Islam is supernaturally natural and is conceived differently from what one sees in ordinary Christian theology.

When the book of Ibn Tufayl was translated into Latin, it became very popular in seventeenth-century Europe and it became the basis for Robinson Crusoe's story. So, there is a historical relationship, as you can see between the two. Both stories talk about a hero lost alone on an island. However, the metaphysical transcendent element in Defoe's story is totally lost. And it is correct to assume that, in a sense, European civilization was parting in a different direction from the traditional world view. What became important was the invention of tools and physical survival, and so forth rather than principial knowledge. The *'aql* being used to reach God and the knowledge of the Divine does not have a place at all in the Defoe story, but it is very interesting to compare the two.

EL-ZEIN: I want to come back to this comparison between *Hayy Ibn Yaqzan* and *Robinson Crusoe*. I have two questions related to this notion of voyage. First, do you think that one of the major differences between these works/texts is that Crusoe was unable to see the cosmos as theophany, following in this matter a Western perspective on nature? The second question is the following: You mention in *Knowledge and the Sacred* that, "having journeyed through and beyond the cosmos, man, who is then 'twice born' and a 'dead man walking' in the sense of being spiritually resurrected here and now, is able finally to contemplate the cosmos and its forms as theophany." If we can see the cosmos as theophany here and now while we are living, why are we born, why are we going to die?

NASR: These are very profound questions. Let me begin with the first one. Robinson Crusoe's story was written in the seventeenth century when the modern civilization of the Christian West had become more or less secularized, externalized, and, although there were people who still spoke of seeing the messages of God in nature, the *Vestigia Dei*, the mainstream of thought at that time already saw the cosmos at best as a clock made by the divine clock master. The Divine Presence was not seen in nature. In contrast, the living reality of the intellect within man plays a very important role in *Hayy Ibn Yaqzan* as a kind of supernaturally natural faculty which is able to discern metaphysical truth that had been cast aside to a large extent even in late medieval theology and much more so, of course, in the

Renaissance and in the seventeenth century. Consequently, you have two very different worlds within which *Hayy Ibn Yaqzan*, on the one hand, and the Robinson Crusoe story, on the other hand, take place, although the second is very much influenced on the external level by the first.

You were right in saying that for Robinson Crusoe nature is simply a set of objects out there to be used and manipulated for the needs of man, and thus Robinson Crusoe is able to survive and live although being alone on an island, whereas for *Hayy Ibn Yaqzan*, nature is there not only as a set of objects, things to be used and manipulated, but also as a kind of participant with Hayy in the discovery of truth, truth in the religious and sacred sense, not only the objective scientific truth in the modern sense. Therefore, neither the subjective inner element where the microcosmic intellect resides nor the objective world which is the world of nature is cut off from what we would call the supernatural in the story of Hayy, in contrast to how nature and supernature, or the natural and the supernatural, are made distinct from each other in the context of the Robinson Crusoe story, which also does not deal as much with religion and philosophy as does Ibn Tufayl's tale.

In fact, this distinction goes farther back, I think, to before the seventeenth century. There is in general, one might say, a tendency in Christian theology to draw a stronger line of separation between the natural and the supernatural than in the Islamic religion and religious thoughts. For example, the Islamic notion of *barakah*, which is so central, is not only grace in the Christian theological sense, which is always juxtaposed to nature in Christian thought, but also flows in the arteries of the cosmos, as I have written. And so, in Islam, nature participates in fact in the *barakah*; grace and nature are not juxtaposed to each other.

As for your second question, which is a profound one, the answer would be, first of all, we are in this world to worship God and to realize the cosmos as theophany. We do not start with the cosmos and remain there. We are in this world above all to know God, to serve Him. But once one knows God, one can also know His Creation as theophany. Now, for the first time that one realizes that end, one realizes in a sense that he or she is already in Paradise, for Paradise is theophany, Paradise is wherever you turn, you see the Face of God. Therefore, such a person is in a way already in Paradise although living in this world. That is where the saint is; the saint is already in God's Presence although living in this world. You might say, "Why does the saint then live in this world?" Well, because that is the goal of human life and where God wants him to be. The saint sets in fact a model of perfection for society as to what the goal of human life is. People who realize the truth of cosmic theophany are very important because they affect the ethical and religious character of society as a whole.

EL-ZEIN: How then does "here" oppose "there"?

NASR: The words "here" and "there" are relative words. They are relative to where we are. Paradise is here and now, because if we know what here is and if we know when now is, if we live in the now, in the present moment, at the center, which is here, we are already in Paradise.

EL-ZEIN: Reading the cosmos as theophany is reading the cosmos as a book. And this is another metaphor to which you often come in your books and that I find fascinating. My question is, Do we live then in the Book? Are we surrounded by letters? Do we swim in letters?

NASR: In a deeper sense, yes. From the point of view of Sufism and Islamic metaphysics, the cosmos is the primary, the primordial Revelation of God. In this sense, it is the cosmic book, the *Qur'an al-takwini*. However, as a result of the loss of the perfection with which we were created in *ahsan taqwim*, since we have fallen from the perfect stature in which we were created, *radadnaahu asfal safilin*, because of that fact, we are not able to read the pages of that primordial book by ourselves.

Therefore, God has revealed to us the *Qur'an al-tadwini*, which is the Qur'an as a book. The other "revelations" belong to the same spiritual universe and will, therefore, provide us with keys to read the cosmic book. The message of pure metaphysics written on the pages of the cosmic book is too subtle for us to comprehend without the help of Heaven, which comes through God's formal Revelation.

EL-ZEIN: But what about the *fitrah* in us? Since we have it in us, do you not think we should be able to read the cosmic Book?

NASR: Yes, exactly. Yes, the *fitrah* exists deep down in our hearts. But most of us do not live according to the *fitrah* anymore. Islam is *din al-fitrah* (the religion of primordiality). If the *fitrah* had already been revived, if we were living in the *fitrah*, we would have no need for further revelation; we would have already been there. The fact is that, although we are created by God in the state of *fitrah*, in our primordial nature in perfection, we have fallen into a state where we are deprived of gaining access to it by ourselves. We have fallen away from it. We do not believe in Islam in original sin, but there is *hubut* or fall from that primordial perfection.

EL-ZEIN: Is the loss of *fitrah* a loss of memory?

Nasr: Yes, exactly. *Ghaflah* (negligence) is considered in Islam the supreme sin of *shirk* (believing in a partner for the Supreme Divinity; *Ghaflah* also implies forgetfulness). If we could only remember. And Islam is there to enable us to remember our *fitrah*. That is why *dhikru 'Llah* (invocation and remembrance of Allah) is the supreme practice in Sufism; it is the heart of spiritual practice. All the *'ibadat* in Islam have the purpose of *dhikru 'Llah*, all of them. And once we remember, we can regain our *fitrah*. Then the cosmos reveals itself to us as the primordial book. You see, there is always a relationship between the subject and the object. What an eye sees depends also on whose eye it is, and what is the power of the person to see. The cosmos that God created is a paradisiacal reality; in a sense, it is still here. It is we who are absent from it because of our faults of forgetfulness and negligence. Therefore, one has to consider always the reciprocity between the knowing subject and the object which is known by that subject. Modern science has forgotten very much this truth, believing that the subject is irrelevant to the object that is known, but that is not true. There are layers, envelopes of both the subject and the object, you might say. The cosmos has many layers and many faces, one within the other, and so does our consciousness.

EL-ZEIN: But in fact, the New Physics goes against what you are saying. The quantum theory tells us that the object is not separated from the subject. The observer actively participates in what he observes.

NASR: That is to some extent true, but the Copenhagen interpretation of quantum mechanics, which goes back to Niels Boehr, is the mainstream interpretation. In that interpretation, there is no determining reality accorded to human conscience, a kind of objective status like that of the quantum reality being studied, and quantum mechanics is still based on the Cartesian bifurcation which is based on a subject that is the mind and an object that is the world, and the mind knows the world objectively even if it is accepted on the microlevel that the very act of observation affects what is observed.

It is true that a number of physicists have other interpretations of quantum mechanics. If one can overcome this fallacy of Cartesian dualism, Cartesian bifurcation, then one can interpret quantum mechanics in a way to confirm the idea that the knowledge we have of the external world is based on the interaction between our state of conscience and that external world, and not just the external world itself, which is there independent of our state of consciousness. That point of view is still not accepted by the majority of modern physicists.

EL-ZEIN: In this context of the new physics, what do you think of the book of Frithjof Capra, *The Tao of Physics*? He makes comparisons between quantum physics and the Far Eastern and Indian traditions, like saying that the dance of Shiva is the dance of the atoms.

NASR: *The Tao of Physics* is a successful and popular book. It has had the positive effect of turning the attention of many people to the depth of Oriental teachings concerning the world of nature. However, most of the comparisons carried out by Capra are superficial. The dance of Shiva is not only the dance of the atoms.

EL-ZEIN: It is a cosmic dance.

NASR: Yes, it is a cosmic dance, which is the origin of the higher state of being beyond the physical, which is only the lowest part. But Capra does not bring out the full reality of the traditional cosmologies, especially of China and India. Nor does he deal at all with Islamic cosmology in that book; he has no knowledge of it. When he talks about the Far Eastern and Indian teachings, which are of course very salient, he does not bring out their full reality, their full meaning. I am not at all impressed by taking contemporary physics and comparing it to some traditional doctrine, because contemporary physics changes all the time, while traditional teachings are permanent. What is important is that if you have sacred knowledge based on traditional cosmologies and metaphysics itself, you can always interpret contemporary physics in the light of their teachings to the extent that physics corresponds to some aspect of reality and have a metaphysical and symbolic meaning. One can then interpret it in such a way as to bring out the hidden evidence.

There is a wonderful book written by an American of German origin. He is a mathematician and a physicist whose name is Wolfgang Smith, and the book is entitled *The Quantum Enigma*. This is a book that I think is even more important than the book of David Bohm, *The Implicate Order*. It is an incredible book, which is not known as much as it should be. It came out some years ago, and it deals precisely with this issue. Smith is a man who knows traditional metaphysics, especially Indian metaphysics, and is at the same time an outstanding mathematician and physicist. It is this kind of interpretation to which we need to pay much more attention.

EL-ZEIN: Another quantum physicist, Werner Heisenberg, too, had some insights into the philosophy of quantum mechanics.

NASR: Heisenberg believed that the quantum state represented some kind of potentiality in the Aristotelian sense and the very observation of the subatomic world is an actualization of that potentiality. You have, in fact, not one but two worlds to which people like Heisenberg, even he who is one of the most philosophical among the quantum physicists did not pay attention. Wolfgang Smith, for instance, speaks about the corporeal world in which we live, and about another world that he calls the physical world, which is different from the corporeal one. The physical world is a potential world with which quantum physics deals. Smith mentions that there is "discontinuity" between one and the other, which, in fact, is the result of the act of God, theologically speaking. It is the *Natura Naturas*, which is the Latin term that was used in the late Middle Ages. You have the *Natura Naturata*, "natured natured," that is an active element in nature which actually actualizes the possibilities within the passive and the potential element of nature (*natura naturans*). That, I think, is a profound commentary upon the quantum mechanics: how is it that we observe things and why is it we have this ambiguity, which we then try to associate in a quandary with the determinism principle, and matters like that.

So, there is the possibility of studying quantum mechanics from the point of view of the traditional cosmologies and then understanding certain profound elements of significance that exist in several physical discoveries. Such an answer is quite a different exercise from what Capra has done, which is to take certain Oriental ideas like *yin*, *yang*, the dance of Shiva, and so forth, and say, well, this corresponds to dualism or to the dancing of the atoms. Capra's work is positive to the extent it introduces people to the Oriental world, to the traditional cosmologies. But it is not enough.

EL-ZEIN: Since you mention the Oriental world, what do you think of the way with which the Orient and the West view the science of nature?

NASR: In fact, I have criticized oftentimes the way many people have been studying East and West. They say in general the East is the land of religious metaphysics, philosophy, and mysticism, and the West of science; so we have to combine the two. That, I think, is a superficial appraisal. The East also has its science, the traditional sciences, and those are extremely significant. The West has also had its own metaphysical and philosophical tradition, and this kind of comparison that even some writers from India and, to some extent, from the Islamic world have made, is not profound enough, because in this context what is forgotten is the significance of the traditional sciences of nature and cosmology, which are always brushed aside, even by people from the Orient who try to defend oriental doctrines, saying that modern science has discovered all of these matters about nature and the Oriental teaching in this domain have become outmoded. In fact, they have not become outmoded at all, because there are other forms of sciences of nature that speak about nature in a way which is different from that of modern science. Modern science has definitely gained knowledge of certain aspects of the world of nature. But it also has rejected other aspects of reality of nature and is blind to it in contrast to the traditional sciences of both the East and West. So, I think if we are going to make comparisons, then the element of the traditional sciences and cosmologies should be brought into the discussion and be considered precisely.

EL-ZEIN: To close this discussion on the new physics and traditional cosmologies, how do you separate them? And how do you view the encounter between both fields?

NASR: This is a complicated question you are asking. But let me summarize the response. When I say Islamic cosmology, Christian cosmology, or Hindu cosmology, I mean the application of metaphysical principles to the domain of the cosmos in these traditions. That is what traditional cosmology is. Now, that kind of cosmology does not exist in the modern world view, even among Christians, who for the most part gave it up before followers of other religions. Some Christians are trying to reconstitute it now, but it is not taken seriously by the general public as part of theology or anything like that, because they gave up the cosmos to science in the seventeenth century and the effect of that surrender is still very much present. Catholic Christianity in a sense abdicated its right to know the world of nature, of the cosmos, after the Galileo trial in the seventeenth century. Protestants were never interested in cosmology anyway from the very beginning. Catholicism was, but that was before the Scientific Revolution. Now in the modern world, when you talk about scientific cosmology, and many do talk about it, it is really a generalization of terrestrial physics. We see today a generalization of the modern scientific world view that claims for itself totalitarian domination over any science dealing with nature and over beyond it in such realms as psychology and anthropology. So, we have a completely different situation. That is why this "scientific cosmology" changes all the time. Every ten years there is a new cosmology, like the Big Bang cosmology, the expanding universe, string theory, et cetera. Knowledge of the terrestrial physics is extrapolated for eons and countless light-years, and so forth. It is like knowing a graph for only one inch and then extrapolating it for the next two miles. This is not what traditional cosmology is. Traditional cosmology is not a generalization of an empirical science. It is a "descent" into the cosmos of metaphysical principles which are embedded in the heart of each revelation and each religion. And so, in a sense, the new physics and traditional cosmology are two very different things. The modern world does not have a cosmology as understood traditionally.

EL-ZEIN: Despite the fact that these two domains, the new physics and traditional cosmology, are very different things, as you say, do not you see any hope of bridging the gap, any efforts done by the quantum physicists to come closer to traditional cosmology?

NASR: I think that present modern science is in a very profound crisis, because the classical philosophy, which in a sense underlined it, which grew out of the sixteenth- and seventeenth-century European philosophy and from many other elements, no longer holds sway. It cannot, for it is not sufficient to explain quantum physics not to speak of higher realms of reality. Thus you have a number of physicists who know that paradoxes of quantum mechanics are insoluble within the matrix of the prevailing modern philosophy of science. But they are insoluble so long as you follow Cartesian dualism, which posits complete separation between the subject and objective reality, between the knower and the known. Within this dualism it is impossible to explain the phenomena of quantum mechanics, and that is why you have all these paradoxes. Thus, you find that the Copenhagen School says something, David Bohm says something else, and so forth.

But there are some brilliant and independent thinkers who are trying to bring in incredible ideas to bridge the gap. I have already mentioned to you the author of *The Quantum Enigma*, Wolfgang Smith. There is also a Romanian physicist and specialist of the cosmology of Jacob Boehme who tried to apply this cosmology to the field of quantum mechanics; that is, take quantum mechanics and fit it into another philosophy of nature, into another cosmology than the prevailing modern one. That, I think, could take place. But to expect that quantum mechanics by itself, with its present assumptions, and on the basis of its philosophical background is concerned, is going to lead to traditional cosmology, that is not going to happen. A lot of this New Age synthesis is shallow and meaningless, because, as I said, traditional cosmology is the application of metaphysical principles which are beyond the realm of the cosmos and which cannot be proven or disproven by empirical methods in the laboratory.

In traditional cosmology, whether it be Chinese, Islamic, Indian, Greek, Christian, Egyptian, Babylonian, or otherwise, the cosmos is not reduced to its material part; material component is only a part of the cosmos, and a small part of that. Traditional cosmology always takes into account the vast psychological world and beyond it the vaster world of spirits, angels, and "gods," in the case of Hinduism, and various Buddhas, in Buddhism. For modern cosmology, it is meaningless to talk about the angels or spirits.

EL-ZEIN: I want to come back to this notion of *fitrah* and loss of memory of our previous state from the Islamic perspective. Was not Plato talking also about the same thing?

NASR: Yes. Plato does talk about anamnesis. He talks about recollection. He talks about the forgetting of truths that we should recollect and that is very close to the Islamic perspective, to the *alastu bi Rabbikum* (Am I not your Lord?).

EL-ZEIN: Actually, Muslims used to say that Plato was "Muslim" before Islam.

NASR: That is right. They used to call him *Aflatun al-ilahi*, the Divine Plato. They had given him this title because he was like a prophet who considered knowledge to be the recollection of the Truth he sought to bring out in his dialogues. The whole message of the Qur'an is based on remembrance, to guide us to remember, not to reach something new metaphysically. The Prophet (PBUH) says in a *Hadith*, "I came to bring nothing new, but to remind you of what has always been taught." In fact, we believe that God taught the names of all things to Adam (this is in *surat al-Baqarah*). This means that primordial man contained in his Adamic reality, in his *fitrah*, which we still bear, principial knowledge of reality and the Real. Adam was also taught *la ilaha illa 'Llah*, because he was a prophet. He was a *muwahhid* and had a supreme knowledge of the oneness of God.

And so, for Islam, the role of religion is always to enable us to recollect and to remember. It is not innovation in the principial realm. It is restitution, reconstitution, bringing back to us what is within the depth of our being but that we have forgotten. This point is very important to recall in order to understand the whole perspective of Islam toward religion itself, which on this point is somewhat different from, let us say, Christianity, which emphasizes a new reality, a unique event in history, which is the Incarnation of God in his Son. That is another perspective of religion; it must be respected for itself but as a very different perspective from that of Islam. Many points of theological difference between Islam and Christianity relate to this issue. It is interesting to add, however, that even within Christianity, those who were Christian Platonists believed also in the doctrine of remembrance similar to what we stated above, going back to Clement of Alexandria (d. 215 CE) and Origen (d. 253 CE). But in Islamic thought, this doctrine associated with Plato and Platonism had a much easier task to find a home for itself. Even religious thinkers such as the *mutakallimun*, theologians, who were against philosophers and philosophy, and who might have opposed these matters on the philosophical and theological levels, had to accept what we call here Platonist doctrine because of the text of the Qur'an, which mentions that by teaching Adam the names of all things, God also taught him the reality of all things. The term name as used here does not simply mean John, or William, tree, sky, or mountain. It refers to the essential reality of something.

EL-ZEIN: If we have the *fitrah* in us, and if we are able to see the cosmos as theophany, then we do not need a temple to pray. Nature is our temple. How do you view the relation between temple and nature?

NASR: Virgin nature, yes, it is definitely a temple. Islam, as the last religion of this historical cycle of humanity, joins the primal religions of the world in going back to consider virgin nature as temple. There is a *Hadith* where God addresses the Prophet, "I have made this earth for thee as a *masjid*, a mosque." Now, primordial people, such as, for example, the Native Americans in this country, did not have houses of worship; especially the nomadic northern tribes, like the Sioux, the Cheyenne, and tribes like them. For them, virgin nature was their mosque, church, or temple. When they fought against the white man, the fighting was for their "cathedral" and not only for the land and its riches. While the white man was fighting to gain land and wealth, the Natives were fighting for their sacred temple, you might say.

Now, Islam rejoins this perspective, precisely by emphasizing the *fitrah*. Other religions which require having a temple follow the other perspective, which is that, since we, as well as nature, have fallen from the edenic reality, from primal perfection, we must then create for worship a supernatural space separated from natural space within which the supernatural would be experienced, hence the necessity of building a temple or a church. When you enter a medieval cathedral in France or in Germany, as you come from the outside and enter into the inside, you go from one kind of space into another. The same is true of a Hindu temple. I have been in many traditional churches and cathedrals and a few times inside a Hindu temple. You have a supernatural space inside, which is very different from the outside space.

In Islam, the space of the mosque is the re-creation of the space of virgin nature in the midst of an urban environment that man has created. Its space is supernaturally natural. In principle, in Islam you do not need any mosques for worship if you have access to virgin nature, and that is why, for example, to this day in places like Southern Algeria, Morocco, and the Sahara, where tribes like the Touareg still live a tribal life, they have no mosques. They perform the prayers five times a day. They do all the Islamic rites, but there are no buildings for Islamic rites. But once you have towns and cities, you have need of mosques. Even in Madinah, we had the first mosque because Madinah was already a city in which early Muslims lived. They were not in virgin nature nor in the state of *fitrah*. But since God has given men the power and the know-how to build cities, within that ambience He has also given them the capacity to create a sacred space, and that is why the mosque was built in Madinah by the direction of the Prophet and this edifice became the prototype of the sacred architecture of Islam.

Islam emphasizes the presence of the sacred in all aspects of life and everywhere. The sacred flows within an Islamic traditional city. The floors of the houses are like that of a mosque. Muslims pray on the ground of both. That is why the space of the traditional home is also empty like that of the mosque. It is sad to see modern Arab and Persian houses filled with Louis XIV style decadent furniture. Traditional Islamic houses and the living spaces in them are not cluttered by furniture. In such spaces you sit on the carpet, eat on the carpet, sleep on the carpet, receive your guests on the carpet, rise on the carpet, and pray on the carpet. The main functions of the daily life take place on the floor. Why is that? Because the Prophet (PBUH) put his forehead on the ground on the command of God during *sujud* (prostration) before the Divine Throne during the *mi'raj* as well as here on earth. By that act the ground was sanctified. The Islamic prayers, the *salat* (canonical prayer), is performed on the ground. You prostrate to God in the supreme movement of prayers, as the Prophet did before the Divine Throne. So there came about a kind of sacralization of the floor. Moreover, the floor of the traditional home is in a sense continuous with the floor of the mosque, because you can do inside your house all the obligatory rites that you can perform in the mosque, even the congregational prayer if your house is big enough to hold many people.

EL-ZEIN: How about the roof in traditional Islamic cities? Is it also continuous with the mosque?

NASR: Yes, it is. In the traditional Islamic city, the roof of the mosque is continued throughout the bazaars and living quarters of the city. In traditional Islamic urban design, you did not have one building in the middle and a ground with architecture pointing outward. That is the Western style, but in the Islamic city, in a sense, you have one roof covering the city as well as the floor. So, in a sense, the home is an extension of the sacred edifice, as well as the whole city.

Because of the fall of man, because of the decadence that has taken place, because the urban center becomes also the center for the forgetfulness of God and for extraneous worldly activities, and so forth, the architecture of the mosque was created in such a way as to emphasize the Truth of the reality of the sacred in the whole created order and to remind men of God's primal Creation. For example, inside the mosque there is always natural light that comes in. Air flows from the outside. There is a kind of continuity between the space inside and the world of nature outside; birds oftentimes flow in and out. There is continuity with the external space of the natural world permeated with the Divine Presence. Where it is cold or for other practical reasons, you have to close the door, like in Central Asia or Turkey, where mosques have less direct opening to the air outside; nevertheless, you have in such situations still light of the sun that comes through all the time. You do not have a closed dark space as you have, let us say, in the church or in a Hindu temple.

There is no tension between Heaven and Earth in Islamic architecture as you have in Gothic architecture, which is also very beautiful but has another philosophy. In Gothic architecture there is the "pull" toward Heaven. The space is being pulled upward. In the mosque, there is the repose of the natural world as God created it. So, your question is completely right; in principle, since Islam is *din al-fitrah*, it does not need to have a temple. You and I can go now and do our prayers in the national park of Shenandoah. That is the temple.

EL-ZEIN: So, in principle we do not need to have a temple to pray. But we still have to turn toward a certain direction, to the *Ka'bah*. Why is that?

NASR: Of course, and the reason is very clear. In every religion, the space for worship has to be sacralized. This was called qualitative space. We live in a kind of uniform quantitative space that is based on the Cartesian coordinates and is measured by quantity. It does not matter qualitatively whether you go two feet up or two feet down or to the left or to the right. The modern world has lost the sense of qualified space, which is one of the fundamental principles of all traditional cosmologies and which is related to the question of religious orientation. It is not accidental that in the English language, the word "orientation" has to do with the Orient, where the sun rises. To set yourself right, you have to face the sun. This is what remains of sacred cosmology in the English language, but it is a very universal principle.

Now, in each religion space is sacralized in a different manner. In Islam it is done in light of cosmic reality, because Islam always remains close to the cosmos. There is no sacred text in any religion, except the Tao Te-Ching, that mentions nature as much as the Qur'an does. There, God takes to witness the various cosmic creations of His own. Cosmic realities are sacralized in the Qur'an, and so the living space of Muslims is done in an incredible fashion by emphasis on a vertical axis that relates Heaven and Earth, the axis whose earthly locus is *Ka'bah*.

As you know, according to Ibn 'Arabi and other great Sufis, the *Ka'bah* is the earth's reflection of the celestial temple, and there is a great deal written in Islamic literature on the symbolism of the *Ka'bah*, many beautiful texts written in Arabic, Persian, and other Islamic languages on this issue, into which I shall not go here, but it must be mentioned that by having this central axis and pole for Muslims, every point of the earth is oriented toward it. It is like having a vector field in mathematics. Every point on earth has directionality. It is not only a point like the point here on this table, but it is spiritually oriented toward that one single point which is the *Ka'bah*. I can hardly overemphasize the significance of the *Ka'bah* for the integration of each Muslim's soul and psychological and intellectual inner being and even his or her physical being, because this central axis makes us all oriented toward a single center. Within individual Islamic society, all individuals have the possibility of an inward as well as outward integration with the help of ritual orientation.

EL-ZEIN: Is the function of a sacred temple, not only the *Ka'bah*, but any temple, to reflect a heavenly archetype, to be a copy in some way of a heavenly archetype?

NASR: Yes, of course. All sacred architecture has a function to remind us of the celestial archetype, of the heavenly essences. This fact is true for all sacred architecture, Islamic, Hindu, Christian, Buddhist. They all have a symbolism, which makes the person who understands the symbols and lives within that symbolic world to be both here and there, to be here and yet in the Beyond in the Divine Presence. Definitely.

EL-ZEIN: Discussing the spiritual and symbolic components of the *Ka'bah* reminds me of the beautiful book of Henry Corbin, *Temple et contemplation*. There is a section in this book where he makes a comparison between the earthly *Ka'bah* and its heavenly archetype.

NASR: That book is a profound work. The part of it that deals with the *Ka'bah* is based on the work of a remarkable Persian metaphysician and Sufi named Qadi Sa 'id al-Qummi, who wrote a wonderful book called *Asrar al-'ibadat* (The Secrets of Worship), devoted to all the different Islamic acts of worship—prayers, fasting, and so on. One of them has to do with the *hajj*. And there he describes the symbolism of the *Ka'bah*. It is one of the most profound texts written on the *Ka'bah*. Corbin did very well to translate it and make it available in the West for the first time.

Martin Lings in turn wrote a beautiful chapter on the inner meanings of the prayers in his book on Shaykh al 'Alawi. Every movement of the prayers—the *ruku'*, the *sujud*, the movement of the hands—everything has a very profound symbolic significance. The same is true of the *hajj*. Every single act of the *hajj* has a very profound symbolic significance as well. In fact, if a religious act did not have a symbolic significance, it would not be a ritual. The ritual is what integrates earthly actions to heavenly archetypes. All authentic rituals come from Heaven. They are not man-made. In the case of Islam, a great deal has been written on this matter, and those treatises written on the *hajj* oftentimes include a discussion of the *Ka'bah* itself, and its symbolism. There is, you might know, a book on the science of harmonics as it pertains to the *Ka'bah*, an incredible study done by an American musician, specialist of Pythagorean theory named Ernest McClain. He found that the proportions of the *Ka'bah* are all based on Pythagorean proportions, all of them corresponding to musical notes to musical harmony. It is a remarkable text. This study of the *Ka'bah* and that of Qadi Sa'id al-Qummi are both profound and unique, each in its own way.

EL-ZEIN: Is al-Qummi's text in Arabic or in Persian?

NASR: Interestingly enough, al-Qummi wrote this work in Arabic. He wrote very little in Persian. Let me add that it is very strange that during the Ilkhanid and Timurid periods, before the Safavid era, many Persian philosophers and scientists wrote in Persian, but when Persia became an independent state, many Sufi and metaphysicians wrote in Arabic. The Safavid period is a paradox that could be explained by the fact that many Shi'a from the Arab world were brought at that time to Persia after Shah Isma'il made Shi'ism the official religion of Iran. These Shi'a were brought from Jabal 'Amil in Lebanon, from al-Hillah in Iraq, and from old Bahrain region. Many of them did not know Persian; and there was a rise in the usage of Arabic within the Safavid world for about a century or two.

EL-ZEIN: I want to go back to the human relation to the universe. You often emphasize in your books that the laws governing us and the laws governing the universe are interrelated. You also stress that with this regard Islam is similar to the oriental traditions. Do you mean that we and the cosmos follow the same laws?

NASR: Yes, but not in the modern sense, rather, in the traditional sense. We all have a biological dimension similar to that of the rest of the animals and plants and that is related to chemistry and physics, and, as some say, we have some stardust in our brains, this kind of imagery that is used today. That should not be taken literally, but it contains a profound intuition of the nature of Reality and its manifestation cosmically, even if most of those who use such imagery are not aware of its symbolism, which you can see in various traditions. The laws that govern the world, the cosmos, the natural world have a spiritual and moral reality to them, and not only a mathematical and quantitative character. And in traditional societies those laws are seen as being related to the laws that govern the human world. Therefore, to rebel against the laws which govern us brings about cosmic retribution, brings disorder in the world of nature. And vice versa. This is a basic truth that has been discarded by modern civilization. Nevertheless, many people still have some faith in it. For example, in the modern world some people still pray for rain.

In Greek, the word *nomos* used by Plato means both the laws that govern the cosmos and the laws that govern a normal society, and vice versa. And this word entered into Arabic as *namus* and is used in *namus al-anbiya'* (the laws of the prophets), which refers to the *shari'ah* but the term *namus* refers also to the laws of nature. You have the same situation *mutatis mutandis* in Buddhism and Hinduism, where the word *dharma* is not limited to man. All creatures have their own *dharma*.

Chapter 3

Sufism and the Environment

EL-ZEIN: In *Religion and the Order of Nature,* you stress the necessity of human rituals in reestablishing the harmony between human beings and nature. Are not contemplation, meditation, and poetical intuition sufficient in themselves to bring back the lost harmony? I can sit in front of a lake or a mountain and contemplate it for hours and feel the harmony flowing between the natural order and me. Why do we have to go through the rituals?

NASR: Of course, you can sit in front of beautiful scenery and experience harmony. But that is not the only thing that I have in mind. That of which I am speaking is something much more crucial. To understand what I mean, we have to come back to the meaning of ritual in the traditional sense. A ritual, as I use it in my writings, is not man-made. It is revealed and ordained by God, like *al-salat* in Islam, the Mass in Christianity, or various Hindu rituals. It is not a question of human beings getting together and doing certain actions as rituals that then will have some "magical" effect upon the environment. The function of rituals is to create or, in reality, reestablish relationships between the physical world in which we live and the spiritual world leading to the Divine Reality Itself. Rituals revitalize, you might say, these cosmic correspondences between various levels of reality. Moreover, rituals, by reconnecting us to the Divine, by reconnecting us to our own Divine Center, bring back the harmony between human beings and the world that is the cosmos. There is a triangle that is involved here: the cosmos or the natural world, which is created by God, or which is manifested by the Divine Principle; the human world, which is also created by God; and the ritual, which is a means whereby we are brought back by acts which God had designated to reach this harmony with the cosmos and the Divine. By restoring the harmony with the Divine, the rites restore the harmony with the world around us.

Moreover, the human being has a very special function on the terrestrial plane, which is to preserve the harmony of nature and not to destroy the earth. In so many of my writings, I emphasize this function. No matter how much crocodiles lay eggs in Africa, the species of crocodile cannot eat all human beings there. No matter how fast germs in nature reproduce, they cannot destroy all life on earth.

Our role as human beings is in a sense to receive grace from Heaven, that is, from the Divine Source and to dispense it to the world around them. A society which no longer practices rituals in the traditional sense of the word is no longer able to play that role, and therefore it has a cataclysmic effect upon the environment around it. Now, it is of course possible for an individual to sit down and contemplate a beautiful lake, but even then, the power of contemplation of that particular person is in the long run the result of rituals, whose effect this person has inherited and still bears within himself and herself. Rituals at the highest level include, of course, the essential prayer of the heart, and embrace all those techniques of meditation and contemplation which we find in the esoteric dimensions of the religions of the world, and, with regard to Islam, especially in Sufism. But before we get to the case of an individual sitting down and contemplating natural scenes and feeling harmony with them, we must understand the role of the human collectivity in this matter. We must understand that we function as a community, as a human collectivity, in our impact upon the natural environment. I am not talking here about the effect of the prayer or contemplation of an individual, but about humanity as a whole, which, if it does not perform rituals, in a certain sense it cuts off the world of nature around it from the flow of grace which the world of nature is meant to receive from human beings performing rituals. It is amazing how important this fact is in the creation of harmony with nature. This matter is so much emphasized, for example, in the primal religions, such as that of the Native Americans, where the various rituals are consciously performed by people with the aim of reestablishing equilibrium with the world of nature.

EL-ZEIN: The Sun Dance is an example of that search for reestablishing harmony with nature.

NASR: Definitely, definitely. It is an outstanding example.

EL-ZEIN: Mircea Eliade, in his book *The Myth of the Eternal Return*, speaks of a certain dichotomy between nature and history in Western thought. He specifically refers to Hegel in these terms: "For Hegel, history is free and always new; it does not repeat itself; nevertheless, it conforms to the plans of providence; hence it has a model (ideal, but nonetheless a model) in the dialectic of spirit itself. To this history, which does not repeat itself, Hegel opposes nature, in which things are reproduced ad infinitum."[1] What do you think of this Hegelian dichotomy, and how Islam places itself with regard to it?

NASR: This question that you are asking is a very complicated one, and it can be answered in the following way: The awareness of history, the awareness of the flow of time moving in such a way that we have not experienced before, history which does not repeat itself is considered in later religions but in different ways. The primal religions lived and still live in a kind of space without time. Time is absorbed into cyclic recurrences, which overcomes the withering effect of time that brings with it constant changes, decay, and death. In a sense, then, the cyclic notion of time neutralizes the effects of linear time. But as we move down in the history of the present phase of human life, we see that various religions of the world begin to take cognizance of the flow of time, or what we call history, and the significance of this flow religiously. Why is it so? It is best explained through a remarkable image by Frithjof Schuon. He says that you should take an hourglass and tip it over. You have sand in the upper compartment, which starts to descend to the lower compartment through a narrow tube that separates the two compartments. At first, there is a little flow, and you have no awareness of the significance of the moving of the sand; you would be living in a world that presents permanence, where space is dominant. But as sand flows more and more through that hole, the hourglass begins to manifest the significance of change, of the flow of time, and the more it goes on, the more the older movement becomes rapid; there is an acceleration. This truth is also explained beautifully in the Hindu doctrine of cycles of time. And so in the later stages of this movement of the sand within the hourglass, you become fully aware of the presence of time, which begins to be dominant. The later religions of the world had to be aware of this reality. We find it in Zoroastrianism, we find it in Judaism, which has a very strong awareness of historical time, and this tendency becomes especially accentuated with Christianity.

Now we come to Hegel, who belongs of course to the Western Christian world. But first let me turn to earlier periods and mention that there were certain Christian contemplatives who were sort of Christian Platonists and who understood the cyclic notion of time as well; however, mainstream Christian theology remained tied to a linear conception of time, even Saint Augustine in *The City of God*.

Since in Christianity the Son is incarnated in time, in history, history begins to gain a very important significance even theologically. And as long as Christianity remained strong in the West, this theologically valid view was dominant, and understandably so. Although the Christian element weakened and even disappeared in many circles in the West, the "divinization" of history in a sense continues. Now, it is here that Eliade's comment can be brought in. Traditional man lived in the bosom of nature, in the atemporal and the nonhistorical, which you can see even today among the primal people who still survive on the earth and who follow the primal religions, while modern Western man looks at history as the most significant reality, because it concerns the reality of change and development.

It is very interesting to note that in the context of the monotheistic religions Islam in a sense goes back to the metahistorical perspective. The Qur'an is not a book based on sacred history the way the Bible is; hence the Qur'an's view is essentially nonhistorical even when dealing with elements of sacred history. The events described in the Qur'an are primarily events within the soul. Islam is not so much concerned with historical facts as it is with atemporal truths, and in a sense it reintegrates Abrahamic monotheism into a world which is beyond time, and which is immutable. That is why Islam has stood against this idea of constant change that has been so prevalent in the modern West, even in much of modern Christian theology that reinvents itself every few centuries, then every few decades, and now every few years. Islam does not need to do that. It does not need to redefine the meaning of God every few years. God sits on his Throne and the divine Names are there beyond the transformations of time.

Now, to go back to Eliade, no doubt he was trying to point to the dichotomy between the conception of nature and human history as they developed in Western thought. Such a dichotomy does not exist among people who have a different view of historical time, and that includes not only Muslims, but also Hindus, Taoists, and many Jews. As for the Hindus, there is an interesting story to mention about them. Most of the history of India was written by Muslims, and only later on by Hindus themselves. Historical studies of India began essentially after Islam entered the Indian world. The Chinese, in contrast, wrote chronicles and were very conscious of their history while refusing to sacralize the historical process as it was done in the West. In China there was a strong awareness of the emperor Yu, the founder of the Chinese race, of the Hun people, of the various Chinese dynasties, and so forth and so on. But there was also in Taoism, and neo-Confucianism a philosophy which is very aware of the permanent spiritual dimension of nature beyond history as understood in the West. Human history and nature were never opposed to or separated from each other in China, as is the case in the West, where the divination of history led in its secular form to the view of nature itself through the evolutionary lens.

EL-ZEIN: When you mention that Islam is atemporal and nonhistorical, are you alluding to the Muslim concept of *fitrah*, which brings man back to nature?

NASR: That is right. When Islam returns man to his *fitrah*, in a sense it considers him beyond the accidents of his historical existence, you might say. But at the same time Muslims were of course very aware of history. Islam had many great historians; it is a civilization which is conscious historically but without the theological impact of a sacralized history. This whole Hegelian concept of history to which Eliade was paying attention is particular to Western thought.

EL-ZEIN: Do you not find it stunning that in his *History of Religions* Mircea Eliade says very little on Islam?

NASR: I know. I knew Eliade very well personally, and he was a good friend of mine for many years. He admitted to me that of all the great religions of the world, he knew least about Islam, and that is partly because of the two methods that were developed for the science of religion, which is also called comparative religion in the West. The first method was the historical method, based on the idea of the evolution of religion in the nineteenth century, when this idea of evolution of religion came to the fore, an idea that tried to see earlier religions as less perfect forms that evolved into the more perfect doctrine of Christianity. And then, as I already said earlier, this evolutionary idea became embarrassing: What happened to the religion that came after Christianity, that is, Islam? So this approach left Islam out and produced few people who espoused the historical method of studying religions as evolving into higher forms until one reached Christianity knowledgeable or seriously interested in Islam.

The second method was that of phenomenology, which Eliade followed and which he applied to his studies. The scholars belonging to this school of thought were looking in a sense for certain types of phenomena across religious boundaries, let us say kinship or initiation, et cetera. And again they found the whole question of faith in the Islamic perspective and the metaphysics that go along with it to be very difficult to fit into this phenomenological method. That is why the whole discipline of comparative religion produced a large umbrella for scholars in the field of Hinduism, of Buddhism, of the ancient religions, but practically no one in the field of Islam. Charles Adam was among the few scholars who belonged to this school and went into the field of Islamic studies. There is also, of course, the case of Corbin, who called himself a phenomenologist but identified this method with the unveiling of phenomena to reveal the noumena or what he identified as *kashf al-mahjub*.

EL-ZEIN: Another difference between the traditional view of the world and that of the modern West lies in the conception of ethics in its relation to the order of nature. You often stress in your writings what you call "the religious understanding of the order of nature." Could you elaborate on these differences?

NASR: This is a crucial point, which indeed I stress a great deal in my writings. During the last decades, people in the West have started talking about environmental ethics. However, few have realized that ethics has to be related to metaphysics, to the true view of Reality. For example, if you say it is unethical to kill a human being, the question remains why. The answer is ultimately theological: human beings are created by God; they have immortal souls; they have a soul. There is the question of sin, the posthumous consequences of good acts. And if you take the theological and philosophical basis away, what remains? Mostly sentimentality.

Now, environmental ethics is developing mostly based on a sentimental or practical but rarely spiritual and intellectual view of nature. For example, if you say animals have their rights, that is true but what if animals are nothing more than electrons and protons and molecules that have banged against each other for a long time and evolved into animals. The question thus remains: Why should they have rights independent of their utility for human beings? It is this issue that few want to confront. They are afraid to confront it because it challenges the whole modern view of nature and life.

If we believe that human beings are created by God, that they have souls, et cetera, then one should not kill them. But if we believe that they are the result of evolution, then, like animals and plants, there is nothing sacred about them and the often-repeated statement that life is sacred is mere sentimentality. It has no correspondence to reality according to the prevailing scientific world. So, there is no possibility for religious ethics without a universe impregnated by spiritual significance to which this ethics would apply. I have a lot of respect for people who defend animals' rights, but for those among them who consider themselves as secular, there is no firm philosophical foundation upon which they could stand. Why are they defending nature? What we need to do is to take back from modern science the monopoly of knowledge of nature that it claims for itself. It is not true when scientists say, "We alone have the truth about the reality of nature." I believe that religion in the West has to be able to provide once again religious knowledge of nature, a veritable theology of nature. But I do not see this coming soon in the West strongly enough to break the monopolistic claims of modern science. Most of the prevailing Christian theology of nature is wrong in accepting the modern scientific view of creation and then trying to theologize about nature.

EL-ZEIN: Is that is why the Gaia hypothesis might not be enough?

NASR: The Gaia hypothesis is interesting. But to consider the earth to be whole, to be interrelated, is not enough, because it leaves out the wholeness in the vertical dimension. The Gaia hypothesis is a positive step, but it is not sufficient. It neglects not only the spiritual dimension of human beings, but also that of the animal world, not to speak of the Divine Reality that is transcendent and yet permeates the whole of existence, including this world. There is also another world beside the physical that is involved; it is the psychological world. And within us there is the spiritual world. Wholeness means really to understand all the different levels of union and outer reality that are also interrelated. We are still suffering from that reductionism of modern science that is accepting the physical reality as the sole independent order of reality and trying to find wholeness in it through reductionism, reducing the spiritual to the psychological, the psychological to the biological, and the biological to the physical.

EL-ZEIN: You speak at length of the Native Americans' perspective on nature and of other religions as well. Do you think that a better understanding of nature perceived as God's theophany could help us better grasp the transcendental unity of religions, to use Schuon's terms?

NASR: It is a complement to it. Schuon speaks so eloquently about the transcendental unity of religions in his book of that name, concentrating, however, mostly on the human order, although elsewhere he has written in the most profound manner about nature. I have spoken in my books *Man and Nature* and *Religion and the Order of Nature* of the unity to be seen in the view of the various religions of the world concerning nature, or, you might say, the earth. In a sense, in his aforementioned book and also elsewhere, Schuon speaks of the unity concerning Heaven. These realities complement each other. But, of course, the transcendent unity of religions itself could be said to embrace both if it includes the religious treatment of nature.

In order for us to understand how the different religions of the world look at the world of nature, we must first of all understand how these religions look upon Reality itself. What I tried to do in *Religion and the Order of Nature* especially was to show not only that there is this remarkable transcendent unity of religions embracing the Supreme Divine Principle, pure metaphysics at the heart of all manifestations of religious truth, but also how the various religions of the world, despite all the external differences, view the world of nature from a spiritual perspective. There is within that realm also an element of unity despite certain differences, from which we can start in order to solve the environmental crisis, which if continued will result in our destroying the world. Unfortunately, nearly all states and governments and most ethnic groups and societies seem to be in accord on one thing these days: this devastating destruction of the environment.

EL-ZEIN: You are, in fact, pessimistic in *Religion and the Order of Nature*!

NASR: First of all, I do not believe in pessimism and optimism; those are sentimental attitudes; I believe in realism in its medieval sense. Moreover, I think that when a person believes ultimately in the reality of the spiritual world, he cannot be pessimistic. But I am certainly very concerned about the way we are going about dealing with our environment. The god of technology is today dominating the whole globe, and it is being worshiped by the majority of human beings without concern about the massive destruction of the earth, although there are of course those who are deeply concerned with it. Otherwise, there would be no environmental movements. We are increasing our negative impact upon the natural environment every day, disregarding the consequences and usually proposing cosmetic solutions. In that sense, I always say that the only hope is in a major natural catastrophe.

EL-ZEIN: What kind of catastrophe?

NASR: Environmental catastrophe or industrial catastrophe.

EL-ZEIN: But we had many of those, like oil spilling in the ocean, nuclear plant problems like in Chernobyl.

NASR: That is not enough. That is not enough as you can see by the meager effect they have had on the behavior of modern man globally.

EL-ZEIN: Not enough?

NASR: No, by no means. We hear that three thousand birds are killed somewhere, fires in the Amazon, pollution of the oceans, malformations due to technical nuclear problems, et cetera. Two days later, all of this is forgotten. The same oil tankers continue to sail in the oceans; nuclear plants all over the world continue their functioning as if nothing happened, et cetera. There has to occur a big enough catastrophe to cause us to change the way we live.

EL-ZEIN: A nuclear disaster on a large scope?

NASR: No, I do not mean a catastrophe that would destroy life on earth, but a catastrophe big enough to make people wake up and become aware of the falsity of our ways of living. Otherwise, human life as we know it will soon be over. When a patient is sick, if he has a very high fever, people around him notice it quickly and do everything that is possible to save him, but if he is deteriorating slowly and silently, nobody will notice his sickness and he will fade away. That is what is happening now in the consciousness of most people.

EL-ZEIN: What we are doing in a way is destroying the archetype of Paradise.

NASR: Yes, we are destroying nature, which is the reflection of Paradise. We are committing suicide; we are destroying the future of our descendants. Ecocide will sooner or later lead to genocide and is really suicide.

EL-ZEIN: But in any case, we have advanced so far on the road of technology, and there is no return.

NASR: That is what is always said. I do not agree with this at all. It is a question of choice. We still can make choices. But the more we go down the road we are now traversing, the more we diminish our choices. We need to make here and now very radical changes. We need to stop talking about economic development. Economic development as ordinarily understood is much more dangerous than AIDS in the long run. We keep wanting more and more. It is not only the poor people of Africa and India who are destroying the environment; it is rather most of all the consumers of the West and modern societies elsewhere. Even if you live on an island like those of Japan, you are participating in the process of the degradation of nature. You know what will happen if China becomes like Japan or the US? Can you imagine more than a billion and a half people all having refrigerators, cars, et cetera, and doing what the so-called industrial societies do? It would be a major catastrophe for the environment of the whole earth.

I have a lot of sympathy for someone who is trying to save beautiful bears or birds. Of course, they are God's creatures, and one should do everything one can to save them. But this is not the basic issue. The main issue is that we are destroying the support system of life on earth. Look at what is happening to the coral reefs in many of the world's oceans, what we are actually doing to even the oceans which are so vast. Most people are happy with the technology that they see around them and try to have as much of it as possible, riding big cars, et cetera. But what is going to happen to our children we are leaving behind us?

EL-ZEIN: You criticize the New Age phenomenon severely in *The Need for a Sacred Science*, as well as in *Islam and the Plight of Modern Man*. You do not seem to think that there is any good in it. But it is a phenomenon that keeps growing, especially in America. How do you foresee the future of these movements?

NASR: I think to the extent that the present spiritual impoverishment continues, the New Age phenomenon will be a part of the scene, and I do not see any clear indication of the main Western religion, that is, Christianity and its different branches, filling this vacuum, although there are some hopeful signs here and there. Even Catholicism became more modernized in order to accommodate itself to the modern world and has paid less and less attention to its contemplative aspects, although, again, there are some exceptions. I mean there are a few monasteries, a few movements to turn to for the contemplative life, but the general trend is toward externalization of religion. To the extent that this situation persists, the vacuum will remain. And yet the need of human beings for the spiritual, for the inward, does not come to an end, and is not destroyed by the fact that society at large no longer pays much attention to it. This tendency is combined with the prevalent attitude and mentality of emphasizing consumerism, artificiality, moving upon the surface of things, and lack of depth, which our education and training now in a sense centralizes and accentuates. All of these elements prepare the ground for the continuation of these false religious teachings. Usually, they do not call themselves religion; they call themselves spirituality to avoid the opposition of certain Westerners to religion. Some so-called New Age teachers claim to be spiritual without being religious, and meanwhile they make a fortune. If they at least combined their offering with simplicity and spiritual poverty, it would be less expensive to follow them. The masters of the New Age are able to assemble a large number of followers. Some of them write books which contain a little truth combined with much error, books that are sold in large numbers of copies. I believe that this phenomenon is going to continue amidst the intellectual and spiritual crisis of these days.

The New Age movement came in to fill a vacuum left by the receding of religion in the West. You are right, such movements are usually much interested in the environment, in what they consider to be the sacred quality of nature, without usually considering what "sacred" really is and how it is related to tradition and revelation. Consequently, they lack authenticity and religious depth. Their teachings are an amalgamation of elements from various traditions but without depth, authenticity, and spiritual efficacy. Usually the New Age groups are founded by individual gurus and lead to cults. It is in fact very difficult to consider New Age movements without some form of cultism. They try to provide teachings but without requesting the traditional disciplines that these teachings need in order to be efficacious. They unfortunately attract people for the wrong reasons, and even make it difficult for those who are looking for an authentic traditional way within the authentic religions of the world.

There are groups in California who call themselves Sufis but in fact have nothing to do with the Sufism of traditional Islam. If you want to become a Sufi, you have to be a Muslim, you have to be virtuous and pious, you have to pray all the time, you have to love the Prophet, you have to read the Qur'an—none of which is practiced by most of these alleged Sufi groups. They read excerpts from

Mawlana Rumi, often wrongly translated and de-Islamized, whirl like the dervishes without undergoing any kind of ascetic practices and spiritual training. The same situation applies to many of those who proclaim themselves to be yogis or following Zen. Yoga and Zen require specific training, a high degree of discipline, and piety, which many in these groups do not possess.

EL-ZEIN: You mentioned Rumi. I think he was misunderstood in America and became a "gadget" among other "gadgets." He belongs to what I call in one of my articles "the American spiritual consumption."

NASR: What happened to Rumi is in a way similar to what happened to Khayyam in the nineteenth century after Fitzgerald translated his *Ruba'iyyat*. The West made out of him a hedonist and a skeptic. And now is the turn of Rumi to be seen as a lover of God but without the Islamic framework that made that love efficacious and turned him into a saint.

EL-ZEIN: I want to come back to the issue of the sacredness of nature. When you talk about it, you often mention the necessity of a return to the Eastern sciences.

Why is that? And how could such a return help in safeguarding the environment?

NASR: First of all, I mention only the Eastern sciences because the traditional sciences, which existed also in the Western tradition, had been relegated to the margin a long time ago and they became inaccessible. When I talk about resuscitating the Eastern sciences, it is as if I am swimming against the current and against what contemporary scientists think. When people talk about the East and the West, they often believe that the East is spiritual and the West scientific, the East including Muslims, Hindus, and Buddhists. This is a very shallow way of looking at this issue, forgetting the fact that the West also had a strong spiritual dimension before the advent of modernism. The East, in addition to what we call spirituality, is also the depository for the traditional sciences, which have survived especially in the Islamic and Hindu traditions, and to some extent in Chinese traditions, although Chinese communism tried to destroy it. Take for example acupuncture, which is a Taoist science involving the flow of subtle energy. It came to the West, which uses it now in practice, but most Westerners do not think about grounding it in its cosmological foundation, which is of course very important. The strange fact to consider in America is that many people are religious in practice, but in the mental outlook they are secular. It is a very strange phenomenon. So even these Eastern sciences are brought here as practices, but few want to consider the intellectual worldview in which they are based.

I have been speaking and writing for more than fifty years about the need to have another category, not just of science and religion and this division that stipulates that the sacred belongs to religion and the secular to science, but of a science that has a religious aspect and a religion that is also concerned with science.

To have sacred science, you cannot start from scratch. We have to go back and rediscover these old traditions that have existed in various religious cultures of the world, especially in Islam and Hinduism and the Far Eastern traditions. For us Muslims, we have to resuscitate the meaning and teachings of the Islamic sciences; this is not only important historically, but also as a living reality that is crucial for our view of the universe today. I think it is extremely crucial to revive the religious view of nature.

For most religious people, when we say "religious view of nature," they understand it as the world being created by God, and having a beginning and an end, at which time all will return to Him. That is necessary but not sufficient. It is very important to stress the beginning and the end of the universe, but what about the middle? The religious view of nature, as I look at it, means the study of the Divine, which nature reflects not only at its beginning and end, but all the eons in between and, of course, today and now. And that is a veritable science. It is not philosophy; it is not poetry; it is not theology. All these elements are in it, and they are important, but it is also mainly organized knowledge that we call science. I have been kind of a lonely voice crying in the wilderness for understanding what sacred science is and for opening a space in the mental world of contemporary man for it. I do not have many colleagues in the East to help with this matter. In fact, I have more in the West; for example, the well-known mathematician and physicist Wolfgang Smith and the British geometer Keith Critchlow.

However, new interest in sacred science is growing in the East as well the West. As an example, I could mention that my book *The Need for a Sacred Science* has been translated into Turkish, and into Persian, in of all places the city of Qom, which is the center for religious learning in Iran. It is also well-known and often discussed in Pakistan and India, while in Indonesia and Malaysia several works have been written on the subject of sacred science.

EL-ZEIN: You often assert that the environmental crisis is a spiritual crisis and you write that it affects nature, which "participates in man's fall, but not all of nature is corrupted by this fall." Why is nature corrupted by man's fall? Why part of it only? And how do you explain this fall in the context of Islam, which does not believe in original sin?

NASR: First of all, there is no doubt that the environmental crisis is also a spiritual crisis. In a sense, man began to "pollute" his inner space, you might say, and darken his soul within before those traits manifested themselves outwardly. For some time in the West, where modernism began, and then in the eighteenth and nineteenth centuries started to spread to the rest of the world outside the West, many people who were so-called intellectual leaders became agnostics or even atheists, not believing in the primary reality of the Spirit. This whole humanistic, agnostic, and even deistic wave, which led to all kinds of materialism, darkened the inner space of man, if I can use this image. And it was only later that it began to manifest itself outwardly in a noticeable way. Even in the nineteenth century, some of the proponents of materialistic philosophies, such as Marxism, were living in places that were green, filled with trees and in the bosom of serene nature. They were not aware that their ideas would affect nature that surrounded them. But they did. By controlling nature and dominating it, modern technology, which is an application of materialistic science, cut both man and nature off from their Divine Origin. Modern man himself became like a god dominating nature, and the science of nature was established on the basis of the secular alone, along with modern technologies of nature. All these developments went hand in hand to allow the devastation of the world of nature that we observe. There is no doubt about that fact. The inner plight of man comes before his outer plight and the devastation of the world of nature. This is the very reason why it is not possible to solve the environmental problem without solving the problem within us. As I say at the end of my book *Man and Nature*, in order for man to be at peace with the earth, he needs to be at peace with Heaven. There is no other way of doing it.

As for the second part of your question, regarding the fall of man and nature, of course Islam does not believe in original sin, but it does believe that man has fallen. There is *hubut* from the state of perfection which Adam lived when he was in Paradise. Paradise is the prototype of the world of nature, and before the fall Adam saw God everywhere that he looked. But he did fall on earth, and lost that original vision, and, in a sense, nature also participated in that fall, but not to the same extent as man. Now, Islam always tries to emphasize the importance of nature as God's creation and even nature's participation in the Qur'anic Revelation. The Qur'an not only addresses both the worlds of men and jinn, but also nature, such as the moon, the sun, mountains, bees, ants, et cetera, which are often taken as witness. *Surat al-Rahman* speaks explicitly of the stars and trees prostrating before God.

From the universal point of view of religion, the fall of man has to do also with man's experience of the hidden and the visible. We see the world of nature according to who and what we are. You could not contemplate the lake or the mountain you mentioned unless you have a contemplative quality within yourself. You see a modern city dweller, for example, who will go to the same lake you are contemplating and play very loud music with his friends because he would be bored looking at a lake in solitude and in silence. Such an experience does not interest him. There is always a reality within that mirrors what one experiences without.

Every stage in the fall of man corresponds in a sense to nature hiding an aspect of itself from man. This doctrine exists in Islam as well as in Christianity and other religions. Jacob Boehme, the Christian mystic, said once, "Nature as paradise is not hidden; it is we who are hidden from it."

As we grow spiritually again, nature reveals other faces to us, inner meanings to us, inner beauty to us. And as we become impervious to the inner layers of our beings, we also lose contact with the inner aspects of nature. We see it as a provider for our bellies and our earthly interests, or at best we see it as a source of pristine emotions.

Now, though nature participates in man's fall, its fall is not total, because nature precisely is innocent and it has not been given by God the power of free will to rebel against Him. So, it guards somehow its innocence and the mark of its submission to the Creator. And although the natural world is old, it has not decayed as we have. That is why nature still provides such a sanctuary for a person who has become aware of the imperfections of the society around him. Go for a walk in the woods, and you will find how beautiful are those trees that we have not cut yet. They bring us closer to our primordial nature, for they have not participated in the fall in the same way that we have.

EL-ZEIN: You talk about nature as if it is always serene, calm, and peaceful. But nature can also be mad, horrible, and the cause of all these ugly and terrible disasters we witness constantly, like hurricanes, storms, and inundations. . . .

NASR: Of course, and it has to be this way, because nature also has the power to be violent, but even that violence aids in reestablishing equilibrium, and calm follows a storm. Even God displays anger when necessary. Violence or anger in the cosmic order is necessary to reestablish harmony and must not be viewed anthropomorphically. Some natural events might appear to be terrible if seen on a small scale, but they play a remarkable role in the harmony of the whole. When a storm strikes, do not look only at the consequences around you, such as falling trees and killing some people and animals, and even devastating a whole area. Look at the larger scale look at what it does for the world of nature in the long run and as a whole. It purifies the natural ambience. It is unbelievable how much the elements of harmony dominate over chaos in nature. A storm is like chaos. But like any other natural chaos, its function is to contribute to the harmony of the total order.

When you go to a forest, you find it beautiful, but there is also violence and what might appear as chaos in it; you see a snake killing a bird, a lion eating another animal, et cetera. There is, however, within all this violence a remarkable harmony, which allows the species to survive together. Our aggression vis-à-vis nature is not like that at all. We cannot make excuses for the way we use aggression against nature by pointing to violent forces and events in nature itself. We have become so terrible in our treatment of nature. I wish we would stop saying things like "He is like an animal." I wish he were. Many among us are much worse than animals.

What we see as evil in nature, like storms or hurricanes that you mentioned, are not evil in the sense of human evil. Nature is innocent of sin. It reflects Paradise and the sacred, and it is a much better guardian of the harmony created by the Source of all beings than we are in our present state.

EL-ZEIN: To be better "guardians of the harmony created by the Source," as you say, could a better understanding of what happened in the Christian West and in the Muslim world help?

NASR: Yes, we could definitely learn lessons especially from what has happened in the Christian West. There were sapiential and gnostic elements in Christianity, but they had become eclipsed by the end of the Middle Ages, partly as a result of the domination of nominalism. In fact, when you look at the structure of Christianity and Islam during the last five to six hundred years, you have many theological parallels concerning, for example, the nature of God as transcendent, the question of human obedience to God, certain moral and spiritual laws, and so forth and so on. But that sapiential knowledge, I emphasize the word knowledge, *sapientia* as knowledge, not simply feelings or even faith, enabled Islam to sustain the view of the universe as sacred reality, as theophany of God's Names and Qualities, and to be able to develop a science of a cosmological order which was not simply a secular and experimental science while the possibility of access to this sapience became less and less available in Western Christianity. Christianity for the most part lost its sapiential and noetic dimension. Even in religious circles it became more and more replaced by some form of rational and secular philosophy, which gradually broke away from Christianity and made itself independent with Montaigne, Boyle, and others. You are no longer dealing with Christian philosophy with such philosophers, although such men came from a Christian background. The philosophy they produced, and especially Descartes's philosophy, points away from a religious philosophy of nature.

In Islam such a process did not take place. Islam, like the other great religions of Asia, the Hindu and Far Eastern religions, did not allow the development of a purely secular science, which is based on the premise that there is the legitimacy of separating a particular domain of knowledge from the Knowledge of God, you might say, from the Sacred. Islam did not allow such a happening; so, there developed many sciences, but in the civilization created by Islam as well as other religions, these sciences were not secular.

This is one side of the story involving knowledge. The other side concerns the object of knowledge, and, in this case, Islam never allowed nature to be considered only a material reality. The object of science of nature was also never secularized, and in Islamic thought nature continued to be seen as the theater of God's creative activity. Consequently, Islam never developed the Baconian idea, based on nature as a secularized reality to be used by man for his own purposes without nature having rights of its own. Muslims did not equate knowledge of nature with utility, useful only for gaining power over nature. The equation between science and power which characterizes so much of the modern worldview was never developed in Islam. Both the question of the legitimacy of the development of a purely secular science and the legitimacy of reducing nature to a purely material reality, you might say, to be manipulated for human needs or benefit, utility, of course, have had a very great deal of impact upon modern view about the natural, the environment, upon how modern man looks upon the natural world.

It is not accidental that the environmental crisis, which is now global, nevertheless began with the consequences of the Industrial Revolution that took place in the West. But that phenomenon did not involve the whole of Christianity, because, for example, Ethiopian Christianity and even Bulgarian Christianity did not play a role in this process. It is in Western Christianity, where gnosis and sapientia were gradually lost and then new philosophies, new sciences arose, but at the expense of forgetting the sacred quality of knowledge and of nature. The consequence of that new view which is associated with modernism was this raping of nature, which began to take place on a large scale from the eighteenth century with the Industrial Revolution, when pollution, along with smoky sweatshops, appeared in England and Germany, and soon elsewhere in both Europe and America. At that time people were only concerned with the human element of the situation, even if they were critical of what was happening. A person such as Charles Dickens wrote very effectively about the terrible condition of sweatshops and children working in factories and mines. Few realized then that this was just the beginning of a vast process of the destruction of nature, the tip of the iceberg, that there would be later much more extensive consequences, which would involve the whole of the environment. Since that time, the time that the Industrial Revolution began, the rest of the world was not polluting nature to any appreciable degree. If the rivers of the world globally and the world's atmosphere were polluted the same way that England and Germany's rivers and air were being polluted at that time, we probably would not be around to talk about this matter today.

EL-ZEIN: Is not this an indication of the differences between Orthodox/Oriental Christianity and Western Christianity?

NASR: This is certainly one of the points of difference but there are also many other points. The process to overrationalize theology, which took place in Western Christianity, did not take place in Eastern Christianity. It is very interesting that the term theologian, in the context of the Greek Orthodox Church, means someone in whom the light of God is present, not what it means in the West. Of course, some Western Christian theologians could also be called theologians in the Orthodox sense, such as Saint Bonaventure and Saint Thomas Aquinas who were both saints and theologians, but generally in the West a theologian has been seen to be a person who talks rationally about theological issues, about God and religion, which is a very different matter from the Orthodox concept of the term.

EL-ZEIN: How about the way modern Muslims treat their environment?

NASR: Modernized Muslims have not been much better either. Look at the city of Cairo or any other large Muslim city today. Modernized Muslim countries are not using principles of Islamic thought as far as the environment is concerned. It is a question of mostly material or power struggle—sometimes for dire political reasons, sometimes because of stupidity, sometimes greed; sometimes all of these elements are combined together. But certainly the programs involving the treatment of nature in most Islamic countries today are not based on Islamic principles about the natural environment and our responsibilities toward it.

EL-ZEIN: Even in medieval Islamic times, the attitude of Islam toward nature was not perfect. Nature cannot be looked upon as sacred in urban settings. Islam, as you know, has always been mostly an urban civilization. How much was this fact detrimental to the environment, and how did medieval Islam deal with nature?

NASR: Of course, every urban setting is in a sense an intrusion into the world of nature. No doubt about that, but there is still a great difference in this matter between traditional and modern cities. The Qur'an says that there is no city which God will not punish before the end of the world. But within the context of having an urban civilization, the presence of the nomads in the Islamic world reestablished a balance between urban setting and nature, as the work of Ibn Khaldun makes clear. Moreover, within the traditional Muslim urban setting and city planning, there were certain environmentally friendly ideas and practices that were used in architecture. For example, traditional Islamic architecture always tries to make maximum use of natural elements, not to go against them as in so much of modern architecture. Take the use of air, for example. These systems that we still have in Iran or in Sultan Hasan Mosque in Cairo where you have air "wind catchers" and ducts for flow that bring air in and out, and cause air circulation are a remarkable fashion of creating air-conditioning without using extra energy and mechanical means, which would bring an extra calamity upon the environment. The use of shade, the use of sunlight, the use of air, the use of water, were all considered in architecture and city planning, and waste was usually avoided. The old Egyptians had plenty of water along the Nile River when the population was just a few million, yet they did not squander water; the population is now over one hundred million, and yet modern practices have not followed traditional ones. So there is not plenty of water for everyone. In medieval times, and even in cities such as Baghdad or Cairo, built along a river, there was always the question of how to harmonize the architecture and city planning with the natural forces and resources and make wise use of them.

Have you ever thought why it is that in the traditional cities in the Arab world, Iran, or elsewhere in the whole Islamic world, the streets are very narrow? Have you ever thought of that? The reason is that in the evenings when the air is cool, it becomes heavier. During the day when it is hot, it becomes lighter. When you have a narrow street, the cooler air, which is heavier, sinks, and when the sun rises in the morning that air is in a sense trapped for some time and the warmer air remains on top; so you have layers of cooler air around you, even at midday. This had to do with careful study of the environment, how to make use of natural forces and elements. In fact, it is remarkable how integrated Islamic urban design was with the natural environment. Hasan Fathi, for example, has brought that fact out and put it into practice in the houses and town that he planned. Even in the use of materials; most of the houses, for example, in Egypt and Iran—I take these two examples as great centers of Islamic architecture—were made of mud, or mud brick, which gradually disappears back into nature. If you abandoned a village, let us say after the Mongol invasion of Iran, if you came back after even thirty years, the village would have receded back into the bosom of nature and trees would be growing up where there were dwellings before. So although there is no doubt that the urban environment always causes some disruption as far as the natural environment is concerned, in the Islamic world this effect was really minimized. And, in fact, one of the truths that the whole modern world, not only Islamic but the rest of the modern world, can learn from this traditional urban design of architecture is its remarkable environmental friendliness, you might say, its integration into the rhythms of nature, and its ability to cause the least disruption possible of the natural world around urban settings.

EL-ZEIN: You emphasize in *Man and Nature* and *Religion and the Order of Nature* that there is a total divorce nowadays between the science of nature and metaphysics. However, we have during our own era some scientists who were concerned about the relation between religion and nature. It is sufficient to mention, for example, scientists such as Bohr, Heisenberg, Paul Davies, to name just a few, who wrote about this interaction of science with metaphysics. Do you not think that the relation between metaphysics and science is expressed differently in each era, that each era invents its own way of dealing with the sacred?

NASR: I do not agree with that assertion. First of all, each age cannot invent its own way of dealing with the sacred; that would not be the sacred anymore. That would be something purely human.

EL-ZEIN: When I say invent, I mean different expressions of, because since science is evolving all the time, the expression connecting science with metaphysics takes different forms.

NASR: If it is the question of science in its relation to metaphysics, this is a complicated issue. There is no doubt that there were and are individual scientists, such as Heisenberg yesterday and Wolfgang Smith today, who were and are interested in metaphysics, but most of them did not know metaphysics well enough (Smith being a notable exception), and they made some mistakes, even including Heisenberg in his treatment of the question of potentiality and actuality, which was pointing to something very profound but did not emphasize the grades of being and verticality such as we find in Smith's works. The recent period has not been like the old days when Ibn Sina was both a great philosopher and also a great scientist. Some scientists do have innate interest in previous philosophical issues; there is no doubt about that, but few have the necessary metaphysical knowledge. Anything that corresponds to some aspect of Reality has a metaphysical significance, with which I would agree. All the way from Newtonian science to Maxwell's equations of electromagnetism to quantum mechanics and relativity, there is no doubt that they all have a significance beyond physics, but that is considered to be totally irrelevant to science itself, according to the modern scientific view. That is why you can believe in God or you can be an atheist and get a Nobel Prize in physics. Physics itself today does not reflect the concern of particular individuals concerning the metaphysical significance of physics. That is the whole problem. You cannot study physics in the Chinese tradition without paying attention to the Tao, yin/yang, complementarity, and other metaphysical principles upon which the

Chinese cosmological sciences are based, whereas today a scientist who is studying quantum mechanics might be interested in the metaphysical significance of it, but many might not. That is why I have always said that in order for modern civilization to survive, you have to reintegrate the modern sciences into a metaphysical perspective, which has not as yet been done in mainstream Western science. So, modern science is considered to be an independent domain severed from the higher domains of knowledge. First of all, in science you are never supposed to speak about metaphysics, theology, religion, or final causes—that would not be considered as rational. If a scientist defines that all the marbles have to be green so anything that is not green cannot be a marble, that is not real science of the nature of reality but that is the way modern science works. Now, if an individual is interested in such a way of looking at things, that might be said to be fine, but that cannot be considered as a complete science. Modern civilization produces a science which claims to be independent of any other order of knowledge and to be complete unto itself. I speak here as a person who has studied modern science for many years. As an individual, you may be interested in relating Paul Davies's physics to theology, but that is as an individual. There is nothing in the mainstream science of physics today that relates it innately to a principle beyond itself. That is the whole problem.

EL-ZEIN: But on the other hand, scientists today cannot be like Avicenna, philosophers and physicists at the same time.

NASR: First of all, this is not always true; they can be. It is the modern educational system and compartmentalization of knowledge that prevents polymaths from being trained, but there are still some of them around, especially those who are both scientists and philosophers. Moreover, what you call philosophy has been itself the handmaid of physics since Emanuel Kant, except for existentialism and similar movements that rebelled against rationalism and that in any case are not relevant to science. You cannot, for example, integrate the thought of Kierkegaard with the philosophy of quantum mechanics, obviously.

Today, a number of scientists who are interested in metaphysical principles of philosophy of nature are studying Taoism and Hinduism; and you have books like *The Tao of Physics* of Fritjof Capra, many works like that coming out in European languages. This is happening because the Western metaphysical view of nature, which does exist, has not been very readily available until very recently. There is now some interest, especially in the last two decades, in the philosophy of Jacob Boehme, the famous German metaphysician, mystic, alchemist, and philosopher, and figures like him. There are a few physicists who have tried to show how his philosophy of nature could provide a philosophy for quantum mechanics, which is much more relevant than the prevalent philosophy of science, which is Cartesian dualism, from which issue all these contradictions that cannot be solved within its framework and are often glossed over. Although the situation is difficult, it is not insoluble. But it is not sufficient to say that every age expresses this relation differently just because some quantum physicists have written some books on the nexus of science and religion at different times. There are certain truths involved that do not evolve and concern immutable principles.

EL-ZEIN: What do you think of the writings of Martin Heidegger with regard to the relation of religion to science, metaphysics, and especially technology, of which he spoke in his article about "the questions concerning technology"?

NASR: I think his critique of technology is very apropos. There are some profound insights to it. The trouble with Heidegger is that he both wanted to reintroduce the reality of being as we have in Islamic philosophy without its authentic metaphysical and religious significance, without pointing to God as Pure Being. There is a contradiction in what he says. When you study someone like Mulla Sadra, you understand what constitute not only the concept but also the reality of being, and you realize that Heidegger is sort of dancing around that Reality without really getting there.

My friend of many years, the late French philosopher and orientalist Henry Corbin, was a student of Heidegger at first, and he translated his book *Being and Time* into French, thus introducing Heidegger to the French-speaking world. It was his translation that first brought the thought of Heidegger to France, and people like Jean-Paul Sartre, Simone de Beauvoir, Albert Camus, and many of these existentialists had read the translations of Corbin. Later in his life, Corbin said to me, "Having discovered Suhrawardi and Mulla Sadra, I do not need Heidegger anymore."

Here is a touching story that may interest you. Once Corbin and I were in Strasbourg together. As you know, Strasbourg is on the border between France and Germany, and nearby there is an old Christian sanctuary dedicated to Sainte Odile, a ninth-century saint who converted part of Northern Europe to Christianity. We were standing on top of a hill, a long tall hill; on one side is France, and on the other side the Black Forest and Germany. And we visited that sight, we stood in front of the church looking down into this forest that goes towards Freiburg in Germany. Corbin put his hand on my shoulder and said, "My dear friend, now I have Shi'ism and a Shi'ah philosopher standing next to me; so, I do not need to go down there as I did in my youth to visit Martin Heidegger." There is much in Heidegger in his criticism of modern technology and of modern science, and those are interesting, but I do not think that his metaphysical foundation is sound. He should have taken the next step and really rediscovered traditional metaphysics and Being as ultimate Reality, which for me is the only true metaphysics and the only ultimate goal of life.

EL-ZEIN: If you were to summarize in one sentence the difference between Heidegger and Mulla Sadra, what would you say?

NASR: I will tell you what Corbin himself said comparing Mulla Sadra and Heidegger. As I said, he had studied with Heidegger many years and knew him much better than I did. Corbin once said something very wonderful to me: "*Al-wujud* (being) for Mulla Sadra leads to transcendence and eternal life. For Heidegger it leads to death."

EL-ZEIN: We live in a very paradoxical era. On one hand, science is divorced from the sacred, but on the other hand, we witness a tremendous amount of books exploring the symbolic world. Many authors have written on symbols across traditions. You are the one who once said, talking about the twentieth century, "This century has been witness to the rediscovery of the significance of the sacred." Do you not think that there is a great hope for a real comeback to the vision of a sacred cosmos?

NASR: Yes, there is always hope. But, first of all, let me make this comment. We are living in a time in which some ideas are dying and some other ideas are being born. What is dying is what is right now very predominant, and most people do not think it is dying, and that is the modern scientistic, quantitative, materialistic view of the world. What is being born is a golden nugget, a golden seed, sacred knowledge. Now, some of the many people who write about myth and symbol make a great contribution to this rebirth, while many of them interpret myth and symbol in a psychological manner, following Jung's interpretation of myth, which is not what myth really is from a traditional point of view. The myth or symbol is like a diamond, like a jewel. In order for you to discover its qualities, you have to cast light upon it. If you are in a dark room, a jewel and a pebble from the beach are the same. As for light, it can come from authentic traditional teachings.

EL-ZEIN: But a jewel can shine in the dark. . . .

NASR: No, there has to be some light. In absolute darkness, it will not shine at all. The reason that I am giving this example is that the light that makes the symbol shine is not the symbol itself; it is the light of the sacred, the light of the Spirit.

EL-ZEIN: Could it be our own interpretation that makes us see the symbol shining in the light?

NASR: No, it is not our interpretation; it is rather our participation in the understanding of that light. Our interpretation does not create that light.

Now, I have much respect for many of the great authorities who tried to revive the study of myths and symbols, even going back to the person who did not have a complete traditional understanding of various religions, but who knew the Western tradition well; that is, William Butler Yeats, in the field of poetry, is open to some criticism, and I am not completely favorable toward everything he says. Nevertheless, he revived the use of many symbols. But in the English language, it is especially Ananda Coomaraswamy who was a great master of this field and who presented a most comprehensive study of symbols drawn from many traditions, at least in the English-speaking world, while René Guénon was writing remarkable works on symbols across traditions in French. These two giant metaphysicians, these two colossal figures, opened up the field of in-depth study of symbols. Many, many scholars in this field who came later, such as Heinrich Zimmer and Mircea Eliade, were deeply influenced by Coomaraswamy and Guénon. Their deepest study of symbols traditionally understood was followed by the luminous works of Schuon, Burckhardt, Lings, and other traditionalists. Some did not want to speak about their influence on them, such as Mircea Eliade, who in any case wrote wonderful books on symbols, such as his *Images et symbols*. It was most of all Eliade who introduced the central role of symbols in the academic study of religion.

The trouble was that this academic interest in symbols became combined mostly with a kind of phenomenological approach in the Husserlian sense, in which you could study myth and symbol all your life without the least interest in revelation and its role in the sanctification of certain symbols, or in the spiritually transforming power of these myths and symbols. You could keep collecting these precious nuggets and putting them on a table and comparing them to each other, without reference to their spiritually efficacious role within each revelation and its unfolding. Let us say, for example, you could study knighthood in medieval Europe and in India, the divine mother in Hinduism and the Polynesian islands, et cetera. You know what I am talking about. There is, however, no way to fully understand the meaning of symbols without the light of metaphysics and the Sacred. I think perhaps the supreme work of symbol in the traditional sense is the book in the last century and entitled *Fundamental Symbols of Sacred Science*, by Guénon, which was not translated into English until the 1990s, which is an incredible work dealing with so many different symbols—that of the cave, of the stars, of the cross, of the swastika, of the circle, of various geometric forms, and many subjects. There is in this work a metaphysical light that is upon them. There is no doubt that, although sacred knowledge can be expressed in an "abstract" language, the Sacred speaks to us mostly in the language of symbols. And that is why all sacred art is symbolic. This is the way I understand symbols—not as signs. Symbols are not signs. The word symbol comes from a Greek word which means to bind something with something else. It is that which binds the phenomena of the external world with the inner and numeral world and therefore allows us to climb from the world of externality, the world of external forms, to the spiritual inner world. Therefore, I agree with you, the revival of interest in myth and symbol is a very important event of the last century in the fields of both religion and philosophy, not to speak of literature and art. Much of this type of study was also misused to land man even more in a psychological labyrinth rather than in the luminous sky of the Spirit.

EL-ZEIN: In this context, what do you think of the work of someone like Joseph Campbell who wrote extensively about myths across traditions and was very much Jungian? Where do you situate him?

NASR: This is exactly the point. Joseph Campbell began his interest in symbols under the influence of Coomaraswamy and later on Heinrich Zimmer. He came to visit Coomaraswamy when the latter was in Boston. Campbell did not practice a religion, and he did not follow a spiritual path. He did not possess that light which only tradition, sacred tradition, can provide, but he had a lot of intuitions, a lot of knowledge of symbols, and contributed to their study. Gradually the study of symbols became like a vast ocean, in which one could swim all one's life without ever getting to the other shore, without existentially reaching the realities that were symbolized.

EL-ZEIN: He was very close to Hinduism, I think; even a believer in it.

NASR: Let us first ask what it means to be a believer in Hinduism in a serious way when one is not born into the caste system, one cannot practice Hindu rites when one cannot get into the caste system. I am talking about praxis, not only respect; yes, he respected Hinduism a great deal. But did he get up every morning at four o'clock and chant the *Vedas* in Sanskrit, and perform the *Pujas* and all the Hindu sacrifices and matters like that? That is what it means to live in reality as a Hindu. Hinduism is not a religion which you can adopt very easily; it is not impossible, but it is very difficult to become a Hindu in the orthodox sense.

EL-ZEIN: So, for you, praxis is essential?

NASR: Absolutely. For access to the sacred, praxis is absolutely essential. Yes, there are exceptions, exceptions to prove the rule, but the norm is always praxis. One has to live a religion and not only accept it intellectually in order to belong to that religion fully.

EL-ZEIN: When we are talking about symbols and myths, it is difficult not to evoke the figure of Jung, whom you and Titus Burckhardt have severely criticized. You have said once that "his psychology is a parody of traditional psychology."

Although I do not want to defend Jung here, for I also have some criticism of his ideas, still I think that he left us a wonderful work on myths and symbols. His work on Mandalas across traditions, for example, or on alchemy, is full of insights. How do you view Jung's role with regard to symbols? I have also a second question: Was not Corbin himself Jungian?

NASR: First of all, let me start with Corbin. You ask if Corbin was Jungian. Corbin and I had arguments ad infinitum about Jung. He was a very good friend of Jung. But his interpretation was that Jung did not really mean by archetypes what he wrote in his books. He meant by archetypes the transcendent Platonic ideas.

EL-ZEIN: I think that too.

NASR: But that is conjecture. I mean you can read Jung. It is black and white; his notion of archetypes is identified with the collective unconscious, which is really "the garbage can" of humanity. And this is where Jung and I precisely differ. Not only I, but Titus Burckhardt, as you mentioned, and many other traditionalists differ from him.

I think that he was also problematic because of the way he lived. For example, he went to India and was in

Arunachala, but he refused to meet the greatest living sage of India, Sri Ramana Maharshi, who lived there. I think that Jung was afraid—to meet such a master.

Now Jung had certain intuitions, and he also had a lot of formal knowledge, having read many works. Yet, I consider Jungianism to be even more dangerous from the point of view of tradition than Freudianism, because Freudianism is openly atheistic and its danger for religion clear, in the sense that it negates religion completely, whereas Jungianism is a kind of parody and subversion of tradition. It is an upside-down interpretation of traditional teachings, which is much more dangerous in a certain sense than their open rejection. I shall tell you why. For us, for someone like Burckhardt and myself, and of course Schuon, who wrote so beautifully and deeply about symbols, for us the symbol in this world is a reflection of an archetypal reality, which belongs to the world of pure intelligibility, of the Spirit, which is above the psychological world. You first of all have to comprehend the reality of ontological hierarchy to understand that truth. In that hierarchy there is first of all God, the supreme Reality, and you have the intelligible and spiritual worlds, which in most traditions are seen as two aspects of the same reality, the spiritual and the intellectual, the *'aqlani* and the *ruhani*, in Islamic philosophy. And then you have the psychological world, and you have below it the material world.

The psychological world is a vast ocean; it is very complicated, convoluted, and elaborate, and itself has many levels. The upper level in a sense touches the world of the spirit. Sometimes in dreams we "see" angels and even prophets. As for the lower levels, they are infernal. Now, for us the symbol is a reflection of the highest level of reality below God. And it has its roots even in the Divine Reality itself, in the level of the Divine Names and Qualities. In Islamic terms you have the Divine Essence, which is above all determination, then the Divine Names and Qualities, and next the determination of Divine Names and Qualities, which is the archetypal world and which contains the concrete reality of the symbol, we might say. In contrast, for Jung the source of symbols is the collective unconscious, where symbols have accumulated over the centuries. Symbols reside in the psyche of various people and have been left there from aeons past. So, psyche has contact with that collective unconscious. Now, this is the very antipode ontologically. Their source is not a transcendent reality and metaphysically speaking of where we consider the symbols to originate from; that is, this collective unconscious, by the very fact that it is collective, implies "the least common denominator," a kind of depository where man leaves his psychological residues, so it is the lower pole of existence; while for us it is the numinous, the luminous pole of existence, that is the original abode of symbols.

EL-ZEIN: I understand your perspective, but I think that what Jung was arguing for is that these archetypes and symbols that accumulated during thousands of years of human life on this earth are psychological residuals that come up in our lives, but they still are connected in one manner or another with archetypal symbols in the metaphysical sense.

NASR: Then why not come out and say so? Why does one have to "beat around the bush"? Jung never goes beyond the psychological realm, does not speak explicitly of the spiritual reality beyond and above the psychological realm. Everything is psychologized and that is false. As for his book on alchemy that you mentioned, you should know the following fact about this one book. Jung was always interested in alchemy because alchemical symbols appeared in dreams of his patients, especially the snake biting its tail, the *Ouroboros*, but he knew very little about alchemy. There was a scholar from Nazi Germany who fled to Switzerland and whom Jung employed and, in a sense, "enslaved" practically. All those manuscripts cited, all those pictures about alchemy, Jung did not know through his own research. It was this scholar who provided him with all this knowledge and the value of that book is mostly in the illustrations; as for the references to manuscripts, that was not done by Jung, but by that fellow.

Now, it is true that alchemy is also a science of the soul, and it has a psychological element to it, but it is not only psychological. To understand Jung's treatment of alchemy in contrast to a traditional treatment of alchemy, just put next to each other Jung's book on it and the book of Titus Burckhardt, *Alchemy, Science of the Soul, Science of the Cosmos*, and you will see why I criticize Jung. I have written on alchemy and have also studied it for many years. Alchemy does deal with the soul but in light of the world of the spirit, of the final wedding between the queen and the king, between silver and gold, all of which transcend both the mineral and the psychological realm, while being concerned with both.

Chapter 4

Sufism and Poetry

EL-ZEIN: My first question is in regard to your collection of poetry entitled *Poems of the Way*. I was wondering which way it is? Is it *al-sirat al-mustaqim* (the straight path)? Is it Ibn al-Farid's way? Is it the Tao? Or maybe it is all of them?

NASR: Actually, let me say something first of all about my humble poetry. I received a very strong classical education in Persian literature. My father was one of the great scholars of the Persian language and taught me many poems of Rumi, Hafiz, Nizami, Firdawsi, and Sa'di. I was, therefore, involved with poetry from the time of my childhood. At the age of ten, I had already memorized hundreds of verses from the classical canon of Persian poetry. Then, in my early twenties, between the age of twenty and twenty-five, when I was still studying in America, I came back to poetry and started to compose a number of poems in English. I said I came back because I spent a few years without reading or reciting poetry, Persian that is, during my high school education and early years at MIT, although I read much English poetry from Donne and Shakespeare to Keats and Wordsworth to Pound and Eliot. At the end of my years at MIT and Harvard, I began to compose a few poems in Persian and English and also to translate a few pieces of some important classical Persian poetry, like the introduction to the *Mathnawi* of Rumi, into English poetry. But I never thought of publishing them. I put them aside and they were lost completely with the Iranian Revolution, and so that poetry from early in my life is gone. Occasionally, during the twenty years I lived in Iran, I composed one or two poems in Persian, not in English, but I did translate a few Persian poems in my English works.

I did not write poetry again until after the revolution. When I came to the West in exile, I was visited by the muses again, and I once again began to write poetry, starting with a poem in Spain that came to me after a serious car accident in Andalusia. My poetry dealt mostly with the theme of nostalgia for my spiritual home, with the theme of spiritual exile, symbolized externally by my physical and geographical exile, and also with metaphysics and spiritual wayfaring, with the Way to the One. Not all of the poems that I have written are contained in my two published volumes of poetry. There are many more in both English and Persian. The verses in this book to which you refer involve spiritual subjects such as the journey of the soul in this life toward God.

At the instigation of friends who insisted that I publish my poems together in a volume, I chose forty of them, which of course are symbolic of the days and nights which Sufis used to spend in a *khalwah*, spiritual retreat. Forty (*arba'in*) is a symbolic number associated with prophecy, with the point of the beginning of the soul's return to God, with the posthumous journey of the soul, et cetera. It also marks the stages of the progression of the soul in Sufism. And so the number of poems chosen for this volume is not accidental but symbolic. Moreover, they are really poems of the Way (*al-tariq ila'Llah*); that is, they represent the journey of the soul through various stages and its experiences but not in a systematic fashion, except in "The Stations of Wisdom," where the stages of the inner journey are treated in a systematic manner.

I named this work *Poems of the Way* to combine the symbolism of wayfaring, of walking upon the spiritual path, which, of course, is the Straight Path, the Tao, the *tariqah*, to which I have belonged since my youth, and also to bring back the specific flavor of Sufi poetry by doing honor to the great poem of the master, perhaps the greatest master of Arabic Sufi poetry, Ibn al-Farid, in his *Nazm al-suluk*, the poet to which you alluded. Of course, the structure of these poems is very different from *Nazm al-suluk*, but still I wanted to honor this great poet, whom I love so much. So all of these elements came together, and I gave it the title of *Poems of the Way*.

EL-ZEIN: Since the Way possesses all of these three meanings, is it then a kind of unity of religions? In one of the poems, you say:

> The Divine seems to veil and unveil itself
> In myriad forms beyond our ken,
> And yet, I see here but the single Face,
> The Face of the One cast in so many veils of beauty,
> In this celestial land of enduring grace.

NASR: The realization of this truth is the fruit of the Way. The Way is not formally the same for all spiritual universes. But I believe that the goal for all spiritual paths is ultimately Divine Unity, the Ultimate Source. When I began the Way, I had an intellectual vision of the unity of all authentic and orthodox paths. I was always attracted to the formulation given by the late Ananda Coomaraswamy that all paths lead to the same summit. And so I would say that Unity is not to be found on the paths, which in fact are many, but at the summit of the mountain where they all meet.

EL-ZEIN: When one reads your poetry or Sufi poetry in general, like Hafiz, Ibn al-Farid, Rumi, Sa'di, et cetera, it is interesting to find so many citations from the Qur'an. In a way, Sufi poetry offers us a "quranization of the memory," to paraphrase the expression of Anne-Marie Schimmel. Is Sufi poetry, then, a footnote to the Qur'an? I am thinking here especially of Rumi's *Mathnawi*, which begins with the line, "This work concerns the principles of the principles of the principles of religion concerning the unveiling of the mysteries of union and certitude." For you is there no Sufi poetry outside the Qur'an?

NASR: Sufi poetry: you call it a footnote on the Qur'an. I would call it crystallizations of truths of the inner meanings of the Qur'an and *Hadith*. It is the expression of the inner dimension of the Islamic Revelation, which did not reveal itself only in poetry. It revealed itself also in other art forms as well; in sacred art, in prose, in music, but especially in poetry. The language of the Qur'anic Revelation itself is poetry of the highest quality, of course, not in the ordinary sense of poetry as it was prevalent in the world in which the Qur'an was revealed. That is why the chapter on the poets (*al-shu'ara'*) in the Qur'an attacks Arab poets of the *Jahiliyyah* (Pre-Islamic period) and criticizes them. Let us recall that the majority of poets in pre-Islamic Arabia were soothsayers who foretold the future for a compensation and were considered to be a kind of "prophet" at that time. So in order to distinguish the reality of prophecy as Islam understood it from the function of those poets, the latter were criticized and denigrated. But, at the same time, the Prophet—may peace and blessings be upon him—of course loved real poetry, and the important point to remember is that the very expression of the Word of God in the Qur'an is highly poetical. A soul cannot be affected, it cannot receive the imprint of the Qur'anic Revelation and also be interiorized and sensitive to the inner meaning of the Revelation without having the rhythm and rhyme of poetry imprinted upon it.

It is not accidental that in Islamic civilization all the literatures pay a great deal of heed to poetry, which plays such an important role. The two great languages of poetry in the Islamic civilization, Arabic and Persian, produced such wonderful poetical works. Later on, many languages of this civilization—such as Sindi, Gurjati, Malay, Bengali, Swahili—followed with much beautiful poetry. To this very day, poetry plays a much more important role in the Islamic world than it does in the West. For example, look at the politicians in the United States. They speak the English language, which is a very rich language poetically speaking, but how many of them use poetry in their political discourse? Whereas you could not go to a meeting in an Arab or Persian parliament or any political or social gathering without sooner or later finding people quoting a poem for you. You can even rarely go to the traditional bazaar to buy a carpet without somebody quoting a poem for you during the transaction.

It is interesting that with all of the different European cultures we have today, some have produced great poetry, such as English, German, Italian, of course, with the sublime poetry of Dante, and Spanish, but it is only in the Spanish-speaking world where poetry still has an important public role. And that is why there are such a disproportionate number of Spanish-writing poets and novelists, especially poets, who have won the Nobel Prize, compared with other cultures and other fields. That is not accidental. It is really due to the still enduring impact of Islamic civilization upon the Spanish-speaking world. Yes, the Qur'an plays a very important role in rhapsodizing the soul, we might say, punctuating it, creating in it this rhythm and meter and rhyme, which then manifest themselves in poetry.

EL-ZEIN: Could you say that this is true even with the erotic mystical poetry that portrays women's beauty? I am thinking here particularly of the great poet, Hafiz.

NASR: Absolutely. Hafiz talks about the beauty of the eyes, eyebrows, cheeks, lips, figure of women, and so forth. His verse seems to use not only the actual imagery and language of the Qur'an but also elements of female beauty. Nevertheless, his *Diwan* is considered a commentary upon the inner meaning of the Qur'an. Hafiz, who was the greatest master of the Persian language, was called by this name because he had memorized (*hafiza*) the Qur'an.

EL-ZEIN: Poetry is about metaphors and symbols. How do you view the difference between the two from the Sufi perspective?

NASR: In the West there is more focus on metaphors than symbols. But what Sufi poets are using is not a language of metaphors; it is primarily of symbols.

There is a very clear distinction between symbol and metaphor. A symbol is an objective, an ontological, reality reflecting a higher reality, the symbolized, while the metaphor is using human language in such a way that one concept or word alludes to another but not usually of a higher order of reality. Moreover, a symbol is part of the ontological reality of a being and is not manmade, while metaphor does not have that ontological status. The language that is used by Ibn al-Farid, by Ibn 'Arabi, by Hafiz, is a language which is eminently symbolic, and which has the power, as symbols do, to integrate and to take you from the divisive mode of thinking, existing, and experiencing of various realities analytically to the synthetic and unitive understanding, to carry you to the inner meaning of the symbol from one level of reality to a higher one. Symbols carry you from what classical Sufis refer to as *al-'alam al-majazi* (metaphorical world) to *al-'alam al-haqiqi* (real world), and also from metaphorical love to real love, which is not simply metaphorical. A symbol is like a bark that carries us from one shore of the sea of existence to the other side. That is why this poetry is so powerful: it carries us with it from one level of existence to another.

EL-ZEIN: When I read your poetry, and that of Sufis in general, the term that comes often and that is really striking is the term "eternity," or eternal. Do you see Sufi poetry in particular as an act of witnessing eternity?

Nasr: Yes, of course. In Islam we had panegyrics, court poets praising various emirs, sultans, and viziers, and so forth. We also have had poetry dealing with mundane matters from time to time. We even have had social criticism in both Arabic and Persian poetry. But the everliving poetry, the poetry that is quoted over and over again, that has sunk its roots in the collective memory of a whole people, and in a sense defines them, that shows the inner dimension of the soul, is always poetry which deals with the eternal realities and values. And that is why its value does not wither with age.

One of the great tragedies that has taken place throughout the Islamic world in the last century is the turning of so many Arab, Persian, Turkish, and Urdu poets to simple emulation of Western poetry and becoming cut off from their own poetic tradition. Even those who are gifted often make up empty phrases, making use of words in their mother tongue, but what is the message? Who is going to read them a century later?

Look, for example, at the interest that is shown in this country (America) for the poetry of Rumi today. It is because of its timeless message. The universality of poetry is always related to its eternal meaning and significance beyond the confines of time and space. It is the imprint of eternity upon it, as you say, that makes this poetry universal to the extent that it deals with the eternal, with eternal values and truths, with eternal issues, with eternal realities.

El-Zein: As a poet myself, I think of poetry essentially as an act of meditation. The more you advance in your meditation, the more you see multiplicity vanish and your words reach silence. How can you explain poetry as an act of writing silence?

Nasr: First of all, I believe that it is not only about silence; it is in the deepest sense the message of silence. All traditional sonoral arts, if they are authentic, arise from silence and lead to silence. There is no doubt about that reality. Now, if we turn to poetry, we realize that the greatest poets, especially Sufi poets, never even claimed to be poets. Rumi wrote specifically, "I am not a poet."

EL-ZEIN: He often ended his poems in his *Diwan* with the word *khamush*, which means, I think, silence in Persian?

NASR: Yes, exactly. It was in fact his pen name. Now there are poets, of course, for whom poetry is simply self-expression, but Sufi poetry is never self-expression. It is rather the expression of the imprint of the Divine upon us. That is what Sufi poetry is. Moreover, the great Sufi masters who have composed poetry have not reached that silence through poetry. They have first reached that silence, and then they have composed poetry which, therefore, brings us back to that silence. Sufi poetry is not the desire for self-expression, for humanistic, you might say, assertion of ourselves, of our egos; it is not about torturing the soul in order to express something which is in our mind.

Real poetry should flow from our inner being, as Plato said. You have to be visited by the Muses; you should not be coerced and forced to compose it without that inner inspiration. Of course, poetry is also craft. You have to work with words as well as ideas and images, like any authentic art. But from the traditional point of view the purpose of poetry should not be to express oneself, but to express the truth.

EL-ZEIN: But a lot of poetry in Islamic civilization was not Sufi poetry, after all. . . .

NASR: Of course. Poetry in general was and remains very central in Islamic civilization. We have didactic poetry, lyric poetry, even grammar and other sciences expressed in verse, such as the *Alfiyyah* of Ibn Malik on grammar, or *al-Urjuzah fi'l-tibb* of Ibn Sina on medicine. It could even be a description of a current event, which could also be done through prose. Poetry is very prevalent in our civilization; and even principles of such sciences as logic and medicine, even *fiqh*, were also expressed in poems, which young students could memorize. As a Persian, I had to memorize verses that would teach me that this word is *marfu'* (nominative case in Arabic), this is *mansub* (accusative case in Arabic), et cetera, instead of reading from a prose book of grammar, as you have in English. So, that part of the function of poetry in Islamic society can be seen everywhere, partly due to the fact that traditional education began by training the memory of the student. It was a way of creating a kind of treasury within the mind and heart from which one could draw all of one's life.

EL-ZEIN: So, in a way, Sufi poetry is almost the only one that is not contrived?

NASR: If by "contrived" you mean having only a practical purpose related only to the training of the mind and for everyday practical purposes, then yes. You have several supreme examples of Sufi poetry which not only express principial knowledge about the nature of reality, but also have the power to transform the soul spiritually. There is a poem in the Persian language called *The Secret Garden of Divine Mysteries*, which I have translated into English. I have lived with this text for sixty years and know it like the palm of my hand. The incredible author of this work is Mahmud Shabistari (d. 1340 CE) who never wrote a poem before this one and never wrote one after this one. When he was in his twenties, he received from one of the great Sufi masters in Khurasan a number of questions which he asked Shabistari to answer. And by a kind of divine or angelic inspiration the whole of this poem descended upon him. In a few days, Mahmud Shabistari wrote some eight to nine hundred verses and completed the work. As one of the greatest masterpieces of Sufi poetry, this work was translated into European languages in the early nineteenth century as Europeans realized how significant this poem was.

There are many other examples of that kind of poetry. Ibn al-Farid is another example. He did not compose great poetry before he became a saint. His spiritual state made this flowing of sublime poetry possible. Rumi is yet another example. In the last century, we have the example of the renowned Sufi master Shaykh al-'Alawi in Algeria, who was a wonderful poet of classical Arabic poetry. He often used to compose poems after Sufi sessions, the *majalis* where the invocation of the Names of God is repeated.

EL-ZEIN: Because Sufi poetry arises from silence and returns us to silence, does it implicate a pacification of the soul?

NASR: Of course it does. Sufi poetry helps us to return to the state of the soul at peace, *al-nafs al-mutma'innah*, as the Qur'an mentions. Sufi poetry is in a sense interspersed with lattices of silence, like in Islamic visual art where you see the pattern of arabesque and geometry, which are defined by empty spaces as much as by the actual forms that are seen through them. Sufi poetry is also like that. It should not cause negative agitation in the soul. It should always create an element of peace, and even if it creates the fire of love, of passion for God, which also must be there, that fire is different from the fire of the lower passions. It is a fire that consumes the ego and brings it to peace and tranquility, which is that silence about which you speak. No one can write authentic Sufi poetry without having discovered the silent center in his or her own being.

EL-ZEIN: Is not this one of the great paradoxes of the Logos—that we create silence through the use of words?

NASR: Yes. In fact, it is a great miracle. According to traditional theories, the word arose from silence, and then humanity first began to speak in poetry, and then only later in prose. Use of prose is a form of fall from the ubiquitous use of poetry. You might ask why it is so. It is because the impact of the Logos upon the soul was at first much more firm, before our fall through various stages of history, and that is why archaic languages are much more poetical than later languages. Unfortunately, some of these archaic languages died out as everyday languages, like, for example, Sanskrit. There are a few thousand families left in India who still speak Sanskrit, and of course there are some scholars who do so. The Logos, when it manifests itself, always comes in a highly poetical language. It is not accidental that the sacred scriptures of the world are called great literature and they are so poetical.

We read the Bible in English today instead of reading it in the original language. Christ spoke Aramaic, but the New Testament was recorded in Greek. But in Arabic, we have in the Qur'an the original language in which Gabriel spoke. He did not and could not have spoken in a prosaic manner. It is noteworthy to remember that the adjective "prosaic" in English has this pejorative aspect to it.

EL-ZEIN: Could we say then that poetry is more central in the Muslim world because it remained closer to the origin of things that were expressed through the Logos, while the West distanced itself from the origin because Christ's words in the New Testament were recorded in Greek and not Aramaic?

NASR: That is one of the reasons. But there is a second reason that is even more important: that is, in religions where you have a single sacred text, which is extremely central, revered, and often memorized in the original sacred language, such as the Qur'an is in the Islamic world, its impact is not only historical; it is perpetual. Every generation of Muslims, every young child is taught to read, let us say, *surat al-waqi'ah*, which has unbelievable musical and poetic quality, the impact of which is therefore perpetuated and is repeated with every generation.

There is another reason why the weakening of poetry happened in Europe in contrast to the Islamic world. It is that poetry reflects, of course, the state of the soul more than any other art. Therefore, as the European mind became more and more divorced from the intellectual in the sense that I use this word, that is, its luminous aspect, to the more discursive and rational aspect of the mind, which begins in the Renaissance, the poetic dimension weakened and language became more prosaic without, of course, the poetic dimension dying out. This process coincides, in fact, with the full development of most modern vernacular European languages. The first great masterpieces of languages that had already developed before then were of high poetic quality, such as the *Divine Comedy* of Dante, which therefore has permitted Italy to have a stronger poetical tradition than many other Western lands, as every generation has had to learn the *Divine Comedy*. Although the English language started with Chaucer, the secularizing and modernizing effect of the Renaissance did not take root in England until the end of the Elizabethan period, which still belongs more or less to the world of medieval England, of Chaucer, of the medieval English culture, and that is why this period produced Shakespeare, the greatest poet of the English language, whose works mark the peak of English literature. After those peaks, various European cultures became more and more rationalized, the minds of people became more and more analytical and poetry less significant.

Take the case of French. I think that of the major languages in Europe French is the least rich poetically speaking in comparison, let us say, to German, English, Spanish, or Italian. But, at the same time, French developed into a highly proficient analytical language in the hands of Descartes and others. It has a power of clear expression for rational philosophy and thought, which is, we might say, the strong point of the French language, which both you and I know and admire. In the other languages too, there was this great fall from symbolic to more rational expression.

To come back to the question you asked: it is certainly related to the presence of a sacred text and also to the mental transformation that took place in the West, which decreased the significance of poetry as a vehicle for the expression of the Truth. In the modern West the "rhapsodic intellect" was cast aside in favor of the prosaic, and with it the significance of poetry diminished, but of course did not disappear.

EL-ZEIN: This fall from the perfection, as you call it, was interrupted with the Romantic movement, right?

NASR: Yes, of course, there were some reactions to this strong rationalizing trend. For example, in the nineteenth century, there was a kind of reaction against rationalism and classicism of the seventeenth and eighteenth centuries. Thus we saw the birth of romanticism, which attempted to rediscover the soul and the synthetic quality of language and thought, as well as the importance of the creative element rather than the analytical aspect of the mind. Therefore, you have a revival of poetry in many languages. In Germany, you have figures such as Goethe, Novalis, and Rilke. In English, you have the great nineteenth-century English poets Keats, Shelley, and Byron; Wordsworth, Tennyson, and, of course, Blake.

EL-ZEIN: Do you think that one of the major differences also between the West and the Islamic world is that poets have been at the same time scientists and poets, philosophers and poets? I mean the synthetic view of things was behind poetry's thriving in a way.

NASR: This is a very important point you are mentioning. Poetry is not related only to sentiments but also, and above all, to knowledge. The term for poetry (*shi'r*) is related in Arabic to the term *shu'ur*, which has to do with consciousness and knowledge. The root of poetry in English is from the Greek word *poesis*, which has to do with making, molding, crafts, and so forth. This is very significant. This reality made it easier with the rise of modernism in the seventeenth century to take away from poetry its power as being a vehicle for knowledge, while in Islam the situation is totally different. Let me give you an example among many others: 'Umar Khayyam was a supreme mathematician as well as a well-known poet. We do not have one such instance in modern Western civilization. We have so many Islamic philosophers and scientists who were great analytical thinkers and poets such as Ibn Sina, who was at the same time a peerless physician and a poet who composed poetry in both Arabic and Persian. You have the example of Nasir-i Khusraw, Suhrawardi, and Mir Damad, who were major philosophers as well as poets. You do not find this wedding easily in the West. You do not have in the West a major philosopher, such as Descartes or earlier a Saint Thomas Aquinas, who were both philosophers and poets. Today, knowledge in the West is associated primarily with science. But if you write something in poetry, this is not considered as knowledge. It is just poetry, *just* poetry, and the poet is cut off from what is accepted as belonging to the intellectual domain.

There is also an important factor that caused this fall of poetry in the West; it is the loss of vision of the imagination as an ontological reality, as part of the world of objective existence. Ibn 'Arabi speaks about imagination as a creative power. He calls it *al-mukhayyilah al-khallaqah* (the creative imagination). Imagination in this sense is related to cosmic existence as an objective reality. But today it has become reduced to what is devoid of objective reality, like when you say to someone, "You are imagining things." It is equated with the unreal, often identified as illusion.

EL-ZEIN: But it might come back?

NASR: Only if authentic knowledge comes back. Otherwise, even when you have a very gifted poet such as Yeats, he had to reach out to Asian sources for living symbols in order to revive the English poetic language.

EL-ZEIN: Or to his own pre-Christian Irish and Celtic heritage.

NASR: That is right, for that heritage was also grounded in tradition and was premodern. But what was the result? It did not have enduring impact intellectually, because the mainstream intellectual world of the West was molded by the tenet of rationalism and its aftermath and of modern science. So, poetic language has remained excluded from the landscape of the accepted norms of knowledge. Yet, it is coming back to some extent, there is no doubt about it, but it has not transformed the whole English poetic scene. We need only to look to the rise of the "school" of poetry in England associated with Kathleen Raine, who was also a great scholar of William Blake and W. Butler Yeats. There are also Watkins, Keeble, and others in the same "school," who tried to revive the more traditional modes of poetry. But once again, look at the impact of that poetry on English society, how little it is in comparison with the influence of poetry in the contemporary Islamic countries.

The Islamic world has a great advantage in that it is still making use of poetry in everyday life. Every event that takes place which is even politically painful, let us say the Palestinian tragedy, leads to beautiful poetry. There are also a lot of Iraqi poets in exile who write wonderful poetry, and so forth. It is really too bad, however, that so much of this poetry is cut off from the spiritual root of traditional poetry. Among the modernized classes of Arabs, Persians, and Turks, poetry does not play the same role as it does among more traditional classes. Many people even think that there is no such thing as contemporary Sufi poetry. The modern view is that this poetry belongs only to the old days.

Many present-day poets who have become famous in the contemporary Islamic world are people who are simply copying T. S. Eliot, Yeats, or Ezra Pound, or even much lesser poets. They are writing about subjects that do not have any Islamic message. Much of this kind of poetry is not going to last, even if it sounds wonderful. The words of these modern poems are sometimes beautiful. They are crafted beautifully, but it does not have any enduring message.

EL-ZEIN: I want to come back to this issue of poetry and Logos, of writing silence with words. There is a very beautiful article by Corbin entitled "The Musical Sense of

Persian Mysticism," in which Corbin says, "Among the mystical traditions we deal with in comparative religion, Persian mysticism stands out as having intended always towards a musical expression, and as finding its complete expression only in music." Would you say that in general music is the solution for solving the paradox of writing silence with words?

NASR: I would not say it is the solution, because it is possible to have a great poet who is not a musician in the specific sense of playing an instrument, but, of course, not only all music, but all traditional poetry, is musical because of the harmony that it has. Traditional poetry, because of the patterns of *'ilm al-'arud* (science of meters) on which it is based, is imbued with musicality. Now, Sufi poetry, great Sufi poetry, is inseparable from music. Much of it is actually combined with the playing of music, because in the *sama'*, in the *majalis* of the Sufis, music and Sufi poetry go hand in hand. Rumi is the supreme example of this wedding, because he was not only a supreme poet but also a great lover of music whose soul was always in rhapsody. He instituted the Mawlawi *sama'*, which combines dance, poetry, and music, all three together, the *sama'* that still survives in the Mevlevi Order. And in the great *Diwan of Shams-i Tabrizi*, which has never been completely translated into English, you have the most musical work of poetry of the Persian language along with the *Diwan* of Hafiz. It seems almost as if, in the case of Rumi, the rhythms of music are carrying the poetry along. Rumi uses fifty-six or fifty-seven different types of meters in that *Diwan*, whereas, in fact, the use of different meters in other Persian Sufi poetry is within the range of thirty-one or thirty-two only. It is truly amazing; there is no *Diwan* like that of Shams. Rumi does this without breaking the poetic metrics "from below," as most modern poets do, who write *al-shi'r al-hurr* (free verse) and things like that. Rumi remains within the norm of the metrics of traditional poetry, but expands it on the wings of music, which is unbelievable. You cannot read this *Diwan* without almost singing it. So Corbin is quite right. There is a great deal of musicality involved in the expression of Persian Sufism. Of course, there are also Sufi prose works that are musical, and there are also certain types of Sufi poetry which are less musical than other types, especially those that are didactic, such as some of the poetry of Sana'i, from the twelfth century. His poetry was extremely significant, but it is not as musical as that of Rumi, Hafiz, 'Iraqi, or 'Attar and Jami. These five poets I would call the spiritual troubadours, troubadours of the musical poetry of the soul.

EL-ZEIN: With regard to silence and music, I am thinking of Ruzbihan Baqli, who was asked once why he stopped listening to *sama'*, and he replied, "It is God in person who performs a concert for me. That is why I refrain from listening to anyone else who would perform music." I found this to be very strong. How do you read it? Does it mean that if we are attuned to the Divine music, we are not anymore in need of human music?

NASR: That is right. Ruzbihan wrote some of the most beautiful pages on the spiritual significance of music, some of which I translated myself in my book *Islamic Art and Spirituality*. It was not that he was not sensitive to the significance of *sama'*, but what he says is of course that the highest form of *sama'* is the music that we might say God plays, for God is also the supreme musician. Rumi has a wonderful verse in which he says, "We are like the harp which Thou pluckest." In a sense we are ourselves the instruments that God plays, and when one reaches that stage of spiritual perfection, yes, one does not need the external *sama'*.

EL-ZEIN: Corbin comments on the citation in my previous question and writes, "The inaudible was heard by him as pure inner music." Is this the same music that you talk about in your poem precisely entitled *Silent Music*, where you say:

> For when the heart recalls the Friend,
> That music rends asunder the veil,
> And flows from our being, a luminous sound,
> Silent to the outward ear,
> Yet heard by those whose hearing is attuned
> To the undying melody of that silent music.

NASR: It certainly is. As you know, in the both mystical and philosophical traditions of Islam and the West there is this reference to silent music, which Ruzbihan spoke about, as well as Saint John of the Cross. It goes back to the famous description by Plato of the silent music which is only heard by the sages, and this is a very profound doctrine concerning not only the origin of music and kinds of music but also the relationship between, we might say, purely spiritual music, which is the unmanifested prototype of music, and ordinary audible music. The unmanifested is not heard; therefore it is silent from the point of view of the external world in which we live, but at the same time it manifests itself within all great music, all spiritual music, let us say classical Arabic or Persian music or the music of the Mevlevi Order in Turkey and the Gregorian Chant in the West, which, when you listen to it, in a sense it always pulls you toward the state of silence and contemplation.

EL-ZEIN: Is not this the same music, that of celestial spheres, of which Ikhwan al-Safa' spoke in their treatise on music?

NASR: That is the foundation, the harmonic foundation of the doctrine of silent music. Music has an audible aspect, which you and I hear through the ear. But it is based on certain harmonic proportions, which Pythagoras describes in his division of the cord where he speaks about mathematical proportions and notes of music which we hear audibly. Now, according to the Pythagorean doctrine, the planetary system is also based on music in its relation to mathematics. That is how Kepler discovered the laws of planetary motion, that is, through music and the relationality and proportionality between the movement of the various planets and their distance from the sun or earth and so forth. Kepler was dealing in a sense with musical numbers. And so the sages believe that if you know the mathematical basis of astronomy, not in the modern mathematical sense but in its traditional sense, in the sense of Pythagorean mathematics, which is qualitative mathematics, in a sense, you would be able to hear the inaudible or silent music of the spheres, because you would, in a sense, know the harmonic proportions upon which this knowledge is based. That is one of the profound reasons why the traditional quadriviums are taught in medieval Western universities, which we also know about in Islamic sources as *al-marahil al-arba'ah*, which include arithmetic, geometry, music, and astronomy.

EL-ZEIN: Islamic philosophers also studied music and many were masters of theoretical music, such as Ibn Sina.

NASR: Of course. Ibn Sina in his book *al-Shifa'* devoted a whole section to theoretical music and to proportions in the mathematical aspect of music. In his *Risalat al-'ishq*, he also gives references to music. And, of course, al-Farabi deals very extensively with this in his *Kitab al-musiqa al-kabir*. There is a very deep relationship between metaphysics, the traditional sciences, and music, especially the esoteric dimension of the traditional sciences. This is also reflected, although in a much more external way, in the modern world where usually many mathematicians are very much interested in music. When I studied at MIT physics and mathematics from morning to night, I found that mathematicians, especially pure mathematicians, and theoretical physicists, those who create the pure theoretical models, almost all of them were very much interested in music, and many of them were in fact musicians, but they were not, however, aware of the metaphysical relationship between the two, a relationship that the modern worldview has cast aside. There seemed to be a personal interest among these scientists in music that is much more profound than simple personal choice or accident, because mathematics, even if we do not pay attention to its qualitative aspect, possesses a qualitative reality that is present and is related, in fact, to the structure of music. In a sense, you might say that music based as it is on pure harmonics is like audible mathematics, in the same way that geometry is visible mathematics.

EL-ZEIN: We were evoking Pythagoras a little while ago. How much do you think Sufism as an esoteric and universal path was influenced by Pythagorean ideas?

NASR: Sufism, of course, originates in the Noble Qur'an and the soul of the Blessed Prophet. But because it is the last esoterism of the present human cycle, Islam being the last plenary religion of humanity, it has the power of integration of earlier spiritual messages about which the Qur'an, in fact, speaks. Sufism was able to integrate various existing doctrines and theories, such as Pythagoreanism, Hermeticism, and the like, which were of traditional and esoteric nature, into its worldview. Now, there was already, before the contact with Pythagorean ideas, what we might call an "Abrahamic Pythagoreanism" embedded in the symbolic value of the letters of the Arabic alphabet, *'ilm al-jafr*, which is attributed to 'Ali (peace be upon him), and which we believe he learned from the Prophet. It is a sacred science based on a Semitic alphabet and a Semitic language such as Hebrew and Arabic.

Pythagorean philosophy, however, was just the kind of doctrine, one might say, that appealed a great deal to the Sufi perspective, which is based upon *tawhid*, upon unity, upon intelligibility, because Islamic spirituality, in a sense, is a spirituality based on clarity and intelligibility, not cloudiness, and it is luminous, intelligible, like light that for us is also the symbol of *haqiqah*, of the truth. We can see this reality in Islamic art, from the Taj Mahal in India to the Alhambra in Andalusia. The luminous mathematical clarity impresses the observer. Islamic art is like the crystallization of the mathematical world in its Pythagorean sense. It is not like the dark spaces of the cathedral or Hindu temples. If there is anything that more than anything else expresses clarity and lucidity, it is the light that intermingles with the luminosity of the sun itself during the day. There is an incredible interplay that is thus created. This aspect of Islamic intellectuality and spirituality found in Pythagoreanism is a wonderful vehicle for the expression of its teachings and truths.

Now, this is only one aspect. It is not the whole. There are certain Sufis who were not drawn to Pythagoreanism. Nonetheless, it remained a very important element of Islamic esoterism. And certain Sufis such as Ibn 'Arabi and philosophical writers such as the Ikhwan al-Safa', as well as many others, integrated this element into their teachings. Moreover, especially in the eighth and ninth Islamic centuries there were certain mystical movements, in Persia, Anatolia, and elsewhere, that based their teachings on symbolism of numbers and letters of the Arabic alphabet.

Pythagoreanism in fact had a much more extensive historical presence in Islamic esoterism than it did in the West, where it was quite influential among the builders of cathedrals and many other guilds. But within the Islamic world, it found a home much more easily, because there is an element in Sufism of Abrahamic Pythagoreansm, as Frithjof Schuon called it. This is a very apt and well-formulated expression. It expresses the element of Abrahamic spirituality that accords with the Pythagorean view. This fact is interestingly enough substantiated by the Ikhwan al-Safa' in their treatise on arithmetic, where he is referred to as being *min al-muwahhidin* (from the monotheists). And, sure enough, Pythagoras was a *muwahhid* (monotheist). He belongs, in a sense, to what we call Abrahamic monotheism and to the Abrahamic world based on the Unity of Divine Principle. Muslim thinkers looked upon him as a kind of prophet in the chain of the Abrahamic and traditional prophets, of whom many are mentioned in the Qur'an.

EL-ZEIN: They also looked upon several Greek figures, philosophers and others, as being *muwahhidun* (monotheists). I am thinking here of Hermes in particular.

NASR: Those who were called *muwahhidun* belong to the inward dimension of the Greek heritage. For example, Muslims did not consider the Epicureans or the Stoics as *muwahhidun*. As for Hermes, he was considered by Muslims to be very ancient and associated in Islam with Idris, the prophet. Muslims believed that there were three Idrises, belonging to the age before Plato and even the pre-Socratics, the first one having lived even before the deluge. The texts associated with Hermes appeared around the Christian era in Alexandria with the Greek treatises that came to be known later in the West as *Corpus Hermeticum*. Only later on came the idea that there were three Hermes and not one. This idea was an Islamic one and is not found in the Alexandrian Greek texts.

Among the Greek *muwahhidun* one finds, of course, Pythagoras himself, but also Empedocles, Parmenides, most of the pre-Socratics up to Plato, and, of course, Socrates and Plato. Sometimes Aristotle was added as the tail end, while Plotinus, who was certainly a *muwahhid*, was also associated with this earlier period, this view being the result of identifying the *Enneads* as the *Theology of Aristotle*.

What is interesting to note is that, while the West considers its philosophical tradition to begin with Aristotle, Islamic philosophers believed that Greek philosophy "ended" with Aristotle and his students, such as Theophrastus, because they believed the *Enneads* to be the *Theology of Aristotle*. They did not distinguish clearly the two figures. Generally speaking, Islamic philosophy saw the origin of Greek philosophy to be prophecy. There is a saying in Arabic: *al-hikmah tanba' min mishkat al-nubuwwah* (wisdom

Sufism and Poetry | 153

issues forth from the niche of prophecy). So they considered these early Greek philosophers among the *muwahhidun*.

EL-ZEIN: They even found in Indian heritage several *muwahhidun*.

NASR: Yes, of course. Wherever Islam went, it was the same way. There was the belief that *tawhid* was revealed to Adam, so humanity begins with *tawhid*. It did not evolve gradually toward *tawhid*. When human beings forgot *tawhid* (Unity of God), new revelations were sent to remind them of it. When Islam encountered a great civilization such as the Indian with the very powerful and profound religion of Hinduism as its foundation, they sought to discover *muwahhidun* therein. Some Muslim thinkers claimed to derive the word Brahman from Ibrahim, and they looked at the Brahmas as being the descendants of Ibrahim and his followers, those who preserved the primordial doctrine of Unity. The development that took place among Muslim historians, theologians, philosophers, and Sufis from their encounter with Hinduism is very interesting from this point of view.

EL-ZEIN: I want to bring back the discussion to silence and music since this is one of the major themes of our discussion of Sufi poetry, although some Sufis, like Farid al-Din 'Attar, seem to credit words with immense power, as when he says in the exordium to *Ilahi-namah*:

> Words are the basis of everything
> Do everything with words
> Beg with them
> Ask with them
> Seek with them.

I still find it very frustrating that when we talk about silence, we only produce words, which are unable to create the silence of which we speak.

NASR: The reason for that is that a word evokes meaning; language is impregnated by the signature of the intellect, which provides meaning. Language is like a substance, like dough upon which you impose an imprint when, let us say, you are making a cookie out of it. You see the form or pattern you chose for the dough, as when you put a star or a square form upon it. I give this example because it is simple, and everybody can understand it. Language in traditional theories of language, both Islamic and Hindu, and also in other traditions, but not in modern theories, did not evolve from human beings making sounds like beasts in forests and gradually becoming a Dante. Language in fact descends from above as far as archaic languages are concerned, which are much more complicated and much more perfect in their symbolic power than modern languages. Language did not evolve the other way; it began with imprint of the Divine Word, of the Intellect upon human language. Because of that fact, evoking meaning is beyond the external substance of the word itself. The word is a sound system. It comes out of your mouth into my ear, and it comes out of my mouth into your ear, but it is not only a bundle of air waves. It conveys a meaning that is beyond the material realm of existence. How, then, can a sound system be a means of talking about silence? The answer to it is that there is a place in our soul for that silence, and when you use words, they evoke that meaning that is beyond sound. Therefore, it is possible to speak about silence, which itself is beyond speech.

EL-ZEIN: So, if we do not speak about silence, silence has no meaning?

NASR: No, that is not always so, but words can lead to silence. There are those, as you know, who have spent years observing a fast of silence, which we call in Arabic *sawm al-kalam* (fasting from talking) which complements *sawm al-ta'am*, as we have in the fast of Ramadan. Sufis have practiced over the centuries this discipline. Certain

Sufi orders have even observed *sawm al-kalam* as a means of spiritual discipline for certain periods of their lives, a practice that has tremendous power over the soul.

It is even possible to convey "the music of silence" by just an intimation of the hand, by a glance, by a movement of the eye, by an expression of the face. That is possible, but not always, because we are beings possessed with the power of speech, which distinguishes us from other creatures. It is not accidental that in Arabic and in Greek the terms for speech and logic are the same, *nutq* and *mantiq* in Arabic and logos for both in Greek. Therefore, by using words we are able to convey almost anything; there is no limit. I say almost anything, because language does reach a place where, in fact, we go beyond the world of things and concepts and we reach the ineffable, the indescribable, the unspeakable, and hence silence.

EL-ZEIN: That is when poetry comes in, because it can reach the ineffable and speak about it through images and symbols.

NASR: That is right. The advantage that poetry, spiritual poetry, has over prose and also over everyday speech is that it opens up to the ineffable more readily than prose, which is bound by a system of laws and structures, by a system of concepts. Poetry is much more open to symbols. Symbols are not concepts, which are very different. Of course, prose can also be in a symbolic language. They are not exclusive of each other. But, nevertheless, poetry has an advantage over prose by having a great freedom to be able to express the symbolic, but that does not, of course, mean all poetry is symbolic and of a spiritual character. In fact, much of modern poetry does not have such a trait.

EL-ZEIN: Back to your poetry in your collection *Poems of the Way*. There is a section in your anthology entitled "Those in Quest of Divine Knowledge," which I found very interesting. You wrote poems for Ibn 'Arabi, Shaykh al-'Alawi, and al-Shadhili, the Pole of the age. My question is, What role does a Sufi master play in Sufism in general, and in Sufi poetry in particular? And could there be Sufism without a master, or Sufi poets without a master? I am thinking here of Rumi, in particular in his *Diwan Shams-i Tabrizi*. And finally, how do you view the role of al-Khidr in Sufism?

NASR: No. Let us start with Sufism, and then I will come back to Sufi poetry. Sufism is based on the training of the soul, on untying its knots, on perfecting the soul. Now, if we could perfect ourselves by ourselves, we would not need anyone else to perfect us. So, who is that self or being that can guide us toward perfection? He is the spiritual guide whom we need as a spiritual teacher, a person who already has perfected himself and who himself was in need of someone else to do so, and so on and so forth. This is what we call in Sufism a chain, a *silsilah*, linking one master to another going back to the Prophet. To be able to perfect the soul is a very difficult task. You have to be able to slay the dragon within, as the proverb says. It needs a very powerful spiritual force and human effort to be able to carry out this task. Now, let us remember the basic truth that it is not possible to bring about this transformation without religion, without the aid of Heaven, without spiritual initiatic power, which in Sufism is called *walayah/wilayah*, to which the Qur'an refers. This is a power without which it is not possible to unlock the doors of the heart and transcend the level in which we live ordinarily and to reach the higher levels of being, to overcome the power of the concupiscent and irascible soul. Moreover, we believe that in Islam this power was given by God to the Prophet of Islam and from him to certain of his companions, especially to 'Ali, and also to Abu Bakr and a few other companions such as Salman al-Farsi. Now, only one Sufi order originated from Abu Bakr, the Naqshbandi Order. All the other orders originated from 'Ali, who is the main gate of esoterism in Islam. The famous *hadith* of the

Prophet—peace and blessings be upon him—"I am the city of knowledge and 'Ali is its gate," which is quoted so often, has many levels of meaning, but the deepest level concerns, of course, divine knowledge, which is the heart of Sufism, the attainment of which is made possible by the power that comes from the *walayah/wilayah* possessed by 'Ali and given to him by the Prophet.

Now, for Shi'ism this power is confined to the physical progeny of 'Ali, transmitted by him to al-Hasan, al-Husayn, Zayn al-'Abidin, and so on, but Sufism does not believe that the transmission has to be confined to biological lineage. Rather, it is spiritual lineage that matters, and there were other people, such as Salman al-Farsi and, of course, Hasan al-Basri, very important figures of early Sufism, who were not biological but spiritual descendants of the Prophet and 'Ali. Through such people, initiatic power was transmitted generation by generation. The souls of later Sufis were perfected by this spiritual power, by this *wilayah*. There is no possibility of *suluk*, of spiritual journey on the path (*tariqah*), without the help of this initiatic power, which is manifested in the authentic masters of Sufism.

EL-ZEIN: I have always thought that the Sufi *silsilah* goes back directly to the Prophet and not to Ali. Can you, please, clarify?

NASR: The chain of the orders (except the Naqshbandiyyah) goes back to 'Ali, but, of course, ultimately to the Prophet, "the city of knowledge" of which 'Ali is the gate.

Now, there are exceptions that prove the rule. It is possible for a person to gain a high station of sanctity without a human spiritual master. Such people are called *khidri*, those who have been initiated by al-Khidr, the invisible prophet who is mentioned in the Qur'an, and who is seen as a kind of living esoteric function in the Islamic cosmos. But that is not a human choice; that is a choice that is made by God. The human choice lies in finding a human spiritual master. One cannot sit in front of a mosque and say, "I am waiting for al-Khidr to visit me." Yes, that possibility exists, but it is not a possibility over which we can exercise a choice. In Shi'ite esoterism the Twelfth Imam can also play that role.

This path is chosen usually by people who refrain from finding a human spiritual teacher, or people who do not want to face themselves and follow the usual Sufi instructions and so flee to that solution. The case of Corbin is interesting when it comes to this question. He was very much, of course, interested in the spiritual life and in Sufism as well as Shi'ism. One of the reasons he was so attracted to Shi'ism was that he thought that he could follow the twelve Imams spiritually without having a human teacher, knowing that in Shi'ism the twelve Imams can also play the role of al-Khidr. They can be spiritual guides for certain people, and there are certain prayers that you can perform to have a vision of them. So Corbin was a person like that, and we would have discussions about this matter together.

EL-ZEIN: Did not Corbin remain in his Protestant faith until the end of his days?

NASR: Only outwardly. Inwardly he considered himself a Shi'ite and would often say, "Nous Shi'ites" (we Shi'ites). But let me return to the question of the spiritual master in general and say again that direct spiritual guidance by the Imams or al-Khidr are exceptions that prove the rule. The rule is that in order to advance on the spiritual path one must have a spiritual teacher. Bayazid al-Bastami, the famous Sufi from Khurasan, once said, "Those who do not have a spiritual master have the devil as their master." He didn't say that every Muslim had to have a spiritual master, but those who want to walk upon the spiritual path must have a spiritual master.

As for the second element of the question on Sufi poetry, it is interesting to note that Sufi poetry is the fruit of a combination of the realization of spiritual reality of

Sufism and the poetic gift of the Sufi poet. The two do not necessarily have to be present in every Sufi. Let us take the case of someone like Jalal al-Din Rumi, who is one of the foremost traditional poets and certainly one of the greatest of the Persian language. His father was an accomplished Sufi, Baha' al-Din Walad, but he was not a poet, although his father was his first spiritual teacher. Rumi also had other spiritual teachers before he met Shams-i Tabrizi. I do not believe that Shams was the spiritual teacher of Rumi. I have written about that matter elsewhere. I can use this image on his encounter with Rumi: Shams was like a comet that came to the sky of the life of Rumi. When a comet nears the sea, it produces waves, and similarly this encounter produced waves in the soul of Rumi, and these waves produced incredible poetry.

Now, Shams was not a poet, and, in fact, none of Rumi's spiritual teachers were known as poets. So, to answer your question: it is not that a Sufi poet must have a spiritual teacher who is also a Sufi poet in order to become a Sufi poet. You can have a teacher who is a great Sufi poet, but you can become very advanced without becoming a poet and vice versa. Ibn 'Arabi, for example, had many spiritual teachers in Andalusia; we know their names. None of them was known to be a great poet. The same thing happened with Ibn al-Farid. Most great Sufi masters in the last few centuries have also written some poetry. Some of them were great poets and some not so. But, in general, few of them were very great poets like Rumi.

Then you have the case of very good poets who were Sufis but not great spiritual masters. The best example in the Persian language is the poet Hafiz. He is really a "divine poet," and he was a Sufi, but he was not a Sufi master or the founder of a *tariqah* (Sufi order) as was Rumi. Fakhr al-Din 'Iraqi, for example, we know his life and his spiritual teachers. He became a great poet of the Persian language, but he was not a spiritual master of the rank of 'Abd al-Qadir al-Jilani, Abu Hafs Suhrawardi, or people like that.

EL-ZEIN: How does a Sufi master recognize or know he is a Sufi master, a spiritual teacher?

NASR: The master receives an inner sign, but this would have to be recognized by others. Moreover, this has to follow usually, but not always, the regularity of transmission in the Sufi order in question. Usually what happens is that the previous shaykh either appoints a number of disciples or only one who has advanced on the spiritual path as functionary, representative, or *khalifah* in the same way that Abu Bakr, the first caliph of Islam, became leader of the early Islamic community after the death of the Prophet. Sometimes there is a difference in opinion among members of a *tariqah* and a search for power; after all, a Sufi order is also a human order.

Ultimately, it is the disciples who have to accept the person who is able to teach them, to be a source of inspiration and instruction for them, and to emanate the teachings of Sufism authentically. In practice the person who becomes the new shaykh should be, then, in agreement with the various disciples or *fuqara'* on the question of authority to guide or *irshad*.

This is what happens on the formal level. However, it can happen that a *faqir* who is neither a *khalifah* nor a *muqaddam*, and does not have a high function within the order, has the knowledge and spiritual realization to become shaykh. In this case, from the point of view of this person, it is actually a sign from God that confirms him for this function. Sometimes you have someone within the order who claims he is a shaykh. In this case, it is the disciples who gradually will discover if he is up to it or not.

EL-ZEIN: In your anthology of poetry, *Poems of the Way*, you refer to the One with multiple Names. Sometimes you use God, or He, sometimes She, sometimes the Self, the

Friend, or *Haqiqah* (Truth). Are all these multiple Names for the One, Sufi Names?

Nasr: Yes, when I talk about God in the poems, those names are present, swimming in the ocean of Sufism. All of the Names which I use are in fact Sufi Names for God, such as *Haqiqah* (Truth), *Habib* (Beloved), He, She, and Friend. We use He and She a great deal in Sufi poetry.

In Iran, a great Sufi once asked me, "Do you want to know what God is?" I said, "Yes." He said, "It is *'U*." *'U* in Persian is a pronoun that could be used for he, she, and it. There is no *huwa* (he) and *hiya* (she), as in Arabic. Sufis also say that God is beyond all pronouns. Everything that exists belongs to one of these categories of pronouns, and precisely because God is God, one can say that He is beyond all these categories, although we can also refer to Him through various pronouns as does the Qur'an.

El-Zein: Like *Hu* (He) in Sufism, right.

Nasr: Yes. In fact, some Persian poets play with the two terms, *'U* and *Hu*. It is interesting that in the Qur'an God uses several different pronouns to speak of Himself. Sometimes *huwa* (He), sometimes *ana* (I), sometimes *nahnu* (We). So, what this great shaykh said to me was like a Zen *koan*.

El-Zein: The most difficult stage on the spiritual path is how to separate the I from the One.

Nasr: That is a very delicate metaphysical point. One has to understand on what level of Reality one is speaking when one says, Thou and I, because God is not only Thou; He is also the root of my I. There are many beautiful poems in the Arabic language that are composed about "I-ness," *ana'iyyah*, about the whole question of *ana'iyyah* in relation to the Divine. The most famous among them is that of al-Hallaj.

On the one hand, *inni*, the I, is a negative element because it is associated with the ego, with the *nafs* (psyche).

Inni must thus be cast aside. Only the Divine I can say I. On the other hand, the root of *ana* or I is the Divine Self, the Divine I. Hallaj paid with his life when he said, *ana'l-Haqq* (I am the Truth), I am He, or I am Reality. His executioners could not understand that he was referring not to his individual I, but to the Divine I at the center of his being.

So, this is a very delicate metaphysical point. One risks being entangled with ambiguities while in fact there is no ambiguity whatsoever if one knows about which level of reality one is speaking. At the beginning of the journey on the spiritual path there is always I am I, He is He, and She is She, the Divine Reality. Then when one advances on the path and reaches intimacy with the Divine, and reaches the supreme *tawhid*, (unity) and transcends all kinds of duality, then one can say: not I, not you, but He, which is also my I in the deepest sense.

EL-ZEIN: Could you comment on the role of women in Sufism in general and in Sufi poetry in particular as inspirers to poets, as poets themselves? Could you comment also on their hierarchy within Sufism? I am thinking particularly here of the Sufi 'Abd al-Rahman Jami who stated that women could occupy a place at every stage of the spiritual life. They could even become the *qutb* (the pole) or axis, which is the highest rank in the hierarchy of the saints. The great shaykh Ibn 'Arabi to the end of his days admitted women to his teachings. And when 'Attar speaks of the light of God in his *Ilahi-Namah* (XXIII), he writes:

"And if it shines for a while upon an old woman, it would make her one of the great ones of the world, like Rabi'ah."

NASR: First of all as far as the role of women in Sufism is concerned, all of the possibilities of Sufism are open to women as they are to men, all of the possibilities, that is the highest levels of initiation, the highest levels of love and knowledge, the highest degree of spiritual attainment, all of the different techniques, different forms of meditation, of invocation; they are all open to women as they are to men. In the *Shari'ah* there are certain restrictions; for example, when a woman is having her monthly period, she is not supposed to perform daily prayers, but even that does not exist in Sufism because the inner prayer, meditation, and invocation can be carried out under all conditions. So, all the techniques and practices of Sufism are open to men and women alike as long as they are qualified to carry out a certain practice.

Secondly, besides attaining the level of sanctity, the spiritual functions within Sufism, the teaching function, the guiding function is also open to women. There have been in the history of Sufism not only great female saints, but also Sufi female teachers. A few examples of such women are mentioned by Ibn 'Arabi, who cites specifically two great women teachers of his own. During the last century we had this incredible woman, Fatimah al-Yashrutiyyah, the daughter of the founder of al-Yashrutiyyah Order, whom I met when I was in Beirut in the sixties. She was an incredible Lebanese woman of Palestinian origin. She wrote a very beautiful book entitled *Masirati ila'l-Haqq* (My Journey to the Truth) in which she mentions my meeting with her. She represents an eminent example of a female Sufi.

Now, you might say why were there not as many women spiritual teachers as men? That is not because of any inner restrictions but is the result of more psychological and social factors. First of all, most women are more attracted to the preservation of the life of the family for which God created them, and so the arduous practices of Sufism appeal to fewer women. But in all Sufi orders there are always a large number of women members. And that has continued till this very day and in fact more so than before.

Then, there is another element to this question. In Sufism itself as a whole there is a very strong element of what you might call sacred and spiritual femininity. In a sense, it is the other pole of sacred masculinity and virility, which we also see in Islam. They complement each other. There is always, in all manifestations of Sufism, something very gentle and feminine as we see in its poetry, in its art, in its music, and Sufism became the great source of inspiration for the feminine arts such as music and poetry. So, there is this perfume of spiritual femininity in Sufism, in all manifestations of Sufism for both men and women. Now, having said all of this, let me conclude by mentioning that in certain Islamic countries, in the Sufi *majalis* women do not participate, but in most Islamic countries they did and still do.

Chapter 5

Art and Sufism

EL-ZEIN: What could artistic forms bring to Sufism? Cannot Sufis do without them? In the history of Sufism, not all Sufis were poets or calligraphers, after all. . . .

NASR: This question should be reformulated differently, because the word Sufism, of course, embraces many different aspects, doctrines, methods, various types of people, various levels of spiritualization, et cetera. I would say that the Sufi tradition as a whole could not exist and manifest itself without artistic forms. That is not possible. Yes, it can be said that the person who has reached the highest goal of Sufism has transcended all forms, and for him or her there is no longer need of form. But even at the highest level for the type of Sufism that deals with the contemplation of Divine Beauty, reflected as well in the mirror of the beauty of the forms of this world, both traditional artistic forms and nature remain a very important element of contemplation. So, I would say that altogether Sufism taken as a whole always has an element of art connected with it.

In the practice of Sufism one finds extensive use of the sonoral arts such as the chanting which accompanies the *majalis*. There is also the art of the dress, which was very well maintained in traditional times; they were very meticulous, wearing proper traditional dress in Sufi gatherings, and even today some of the Sufi orders emphasize that practice, while others have become lax and indifferent to the form of dress of those who participate in their gatherings. The preservation of form in the traditional sense has always been important in Sufism, even if Sufis speak of the necessity of transcending the formal order as the goal of the path. For example, the contemplation of certain forms of calligraphy and geometric design, which are Islamic art forms, is of great importance, and the very ambiance of traditional Sufi centers which were very carefully chosen is replete with them. They have always played a very important role in connection with the creation of the spaces of *zawiyahs*. And so, on all of these levels, Islamic art has remained an important element of Sufism. However, when a person reaches the stage of *fana'* (extinction in God), of course, one has transcended all forms. But then at that stage we might say that the being of the Sufi itself becomes a work of art, the supreme work of art molded by the Hands of the Divine Artisan.

EL-ZEIN: How do you read Rumi's verse addressing God, "We are like the lyre which Thou plucketh?" Is he suggesting that the traditional artist is a vessel in which the Spirit deposits a form? And in this case what role does the artist play? Is he a mere receiver of forms? Is he/she still a creator?

NASR: Yes, the deeply spiritual person is like a musical instrument in God's Hands, because such a person has put his ego and its cacophony aside, allowing the inner harmony to reveal its reality. Traditional art is not about ways of expressing one's individual ego; it is rather a means for embracing and expressing the Truth, which is beyond the individual and for which the individual serves as a vehicle, as an instrument, especially in Sufism, which deals with the most spiritual aspect of the tradition. Let me provide an example. The artist, let us say a musician—I choose here the metaphor and symbol of music on purpose—plays the *'ud* (the lyre) or the *tar* or some other traditional instrument in a traditional way; he is expressing spiritual music, he is creating sounds of a spiritual nature, a spiritual art. But in the deepest sense he is himself an instrument in God's Hands; that is, God is the Supreme Musician who is "playing" him as the instrument of His music. This image pertains on the highest level to the saint through whom God creates silent music.

If we were to become spiritually aware of who we are, we would allow ourselves in fact to be the lyre, as Rumi says, which God pluckest. Actually, what would then emanate from us would be like the musical sound coming out of the lyre, out of a musical instrument. It would be a sound that is beautiful because God is the creator of that sound; God would be the creator of that music. There is a passive and an active element involved here. On the one hand, man as God's *khalifah* is active, and traditional art means that he acts and makes things with full awareness of being God's representative, God's vicegerent. But even in the deeper sense, man is passive and it is God Himself who creates art in him and through him, in which case then he becomes in a sense totally dependent on "God's Hands," passive vis-à-vis the Divine Act.

EL-ZEIN: So, from what you are saying, one could say that there is, then, only one artist?

NASR: Ultimately, yes, there is only one artist of real art. As for all that is merely humanistic art, if you accept that also as art, then of course that is something else. That kind of art is an expression of individual egos, and one cannot attribute ego-based individualist forms of art to God simply with appeal to the theological saying that God is the creator of all things. That is another issue that does not pertain to what I am saying here. The question of whether God as the author of all things is also the author of evil and ugliness is another issue that we could discuss later on. Here what is important to recall is that God is the author of all beauty, because He is the Beautiful. All beauty is a reflection of God's Beauty.

EL-ZEIN: Traditional writers in general, Schuon and you in particular, often go back to Plato, and to a lesser degree to Plotinus. Traditional thought seems to have for a task the awakening in us of the Platonic recollection of archetypes. In this sense, art is not creating a totally new form, but rather going back to the original form. In this context traditional writers often talk about the symbol of the mirror. Could you elucidate this emphasis on Plato and expand on the symbol of the mirror in Sufism?

NASR: Let me first answer your first question. There is all this emphasis on Plato because Schuon and I are writing in European languages, and in the Western tradition Plato is the supreme author and the supreme authority for the expression of this aspect of metaphysics, which is to emphasize the reality of the archetypal world that is called the Platonic ideas as reality and this world in which we live as reflection and shadow of that reality. When I write in Persian, I refer to figures such as Suhrawardi or Ibn 'Arabi even more than to Plato and Plotinus. If we were writing in Chinese or Sanskrit, we would draw mostly from Chinese and Indian sources, and we would not have to make references to Plato.

In the case of Islam, Platonic elements were, of course, known to Muslims, and one would quote Suhrawardi, Ibn 'Arabi, Mulla Sadra, and many other Muslim sages in addition to Greek figures. But since one is writing in the West in French or English, and mostly for Western audiences, but also for Muslims or non-Muslims and non-Westerners who understand European languages, the figures to whom one has to allude are men such as Plato and Plotinus, because they were the great expositors of metaphysics, although they did not invent this wisdom. It already was there in the Pythagorean tradition, in the ancient wisdom which the pre-Socratics had already inherited and on which they had expounded, pre-Socratics such as Empedocles, and especially Heraclitus, who talks about the flow of things and showed the nature of this world in contrast with the world of permanence. It was in Parmenides as well. So, this philosophy does not begin with Plato, but Plato is the great expositor and crystallizer, you might say, of the idea of the archetypal realities of which all earthly manifestations are shadows. That is why both Schuon and I refer to Plato and similar figures who followed him.

As for the question of the mirror, that is a universal Islamic symbol that is also present in the Far Eastern tradition, where it had a very important role in the Chinese tradition. Ibn 'Arabi, especially, has said that God created the mirror so that we could speak of His relation to the world. Islam emphasizes very much the idea of *tajalli*, theophany, of reflection of divine realities upon the mirror of "nonbeing," and is not based on the idea of the penetration of divine realities into the material world, which would be *hulul*, or incarnation; that is, Muslim sages have never accepted that the *lahut* (Divine Reality) is incarnated in the *nasut* (the human order). The expression of a saying by Hallaj which implied such a meaning to the ignorant was criticized so severely that he paid for it with his life. The Sufi tradition is very clear in distinguishing one from the other.

As you look in a mirror, you see your image reflected in it. There is a correspondence between that image that is reflected in the mirror and your face as you are looking in the mirror. But at the same time, your face is not in the mirror, and if you break the mirror nothing will happen to your face. There is a remarkable relationship here in which there is both resemblance and separation. The image in the mirror *is* you, because when you comb your hair, you look at the mirror and thereby comb your hair. There is a correspondence, but at the same time it is not you. This remarkable dual aspect which the mirror has is central to the understanding of why it is used so often in Sufism. And, of course, it goes back to the Prophet—may peace and blessings be upon him—who spoke about polishing the mirror of the heart, *sayqal al-qalb al-dhikr* (that which polishes the heart is the invocation of God). The mirror then reflects the Divine Qualities within the heart.

EL-ZEIN: So, in a way, the symbol of the mirror is an expression of the relation between the form and the essence, right?

NASR: Yes, that is true; that is another way of looking at it. It is, in a sense, the relation of the archetype to its earthly reflection, if you associate the archetype with the essence, which is another way of referring to the archetype. But here the word form and essence as used by you must be thought about very carefully, because there are two different understandings of form involved here: one is the Aristotelian understanding of form, *morphos*, which is in fact like the archetype, although Aristotle considers it to be immanent, but is in a sense the essence of something. That is form in the Aristotelian sense. Then you have another meaning of form as used in Sufism, especially by Rumi, in which form, *surah*, is juxtaposed to inner meaning, to *ma'na*, or essence. *Ma'na* in Arabic and in Persian means almost the same thing as spiritual reality; it does not only imply meaning in the ordinary sense. It has another connotation, which is spiritual reality, which could be thereby associated with essence. In that case, then, the form represents the external and the *ma'na* represents the inward reality. So, you have to be very careful how to use the word *form*. For example, when I write on Islamic art or when Schuon and Burckhardt have written about sacred and traditional art, they always emphasize the significance of form. Now, this significance of form is not form as simply reflection; it is the Aristotelian sense of form, form as the idea, as the reality which makes something be what it is. Therefore, it is very important to distinguish between these different meanings of form.

EL-ZEIN: How about the term *shakl* in Arabic, where do you place it?

NASR: That term must not be confused with *surah*. *Shakl* really means configuration or shape, and many people made a mistake in identifying it with *surah*. *Shakl* is not the whole form; it is only part of the form. Form is not only configuration. It includes composure, texture, nature, qualities, and mode of being. All of these elements are parts of the form, but, for example, texture is not part of the *shakl* but is part of the *surah* in the philosophical sense.

EL-ZEIN: Does sacred art in general externalize contemplative states? And how does it transform qualitatively the surroundings?

NASR: Yes, but this is not necessarily the same in all sacred art, but is true in certain types of sacred art. For example, a piece of traditional calligraphy has its own archetype, reached ultimately through contemplative vision, and is then reflected on a piece of paper by the calligrapher. But a contemplative state can be beyond a formal paradigm, in the Platonic sense, which would then be reflected outwardly in forms, except by the void which is formless. For example, the creation of an empty space in the mosque by traditional architects is really the externalization of an inner state, but it is not a form in itself. Also, there is the Zen garden in Zen Buddhism, where you take the elements of nature and combine them in such a way as to transcend ordinary forms, and there is no particular formal paradigm as one sees in the case of the *Ka'bah* or the *Aliph* in calligraphy or the image of Christ in icons, but the externalization of an inner state. In the case of Islam, most of all this type of formlessness is to be seen in the creation of empty spaces in sacred architecture, which are really an externalization of inner silence and formlessness.

EL-ZEIN: What would happen if inner silence were not externalized in sacred art?

NASR: If this inner silence and formlessness are never reflected externally and are excluded from sacred art, gradually a kind of stifling can take place and the sacred art can become cluttered and cut off from the world beyond the formal realm, whereas the function of sacred art is to lead us from the world of forms to the formless. Inner silence or contemplative states, which in the deepest sense come from and lead back to Divine Infinity, have to somehow manifest themselves within the formal domain of sacred art, which possesses, metaphysically speaking, a dimension of emptiness, of nothingness, of nonmanifestation, that are reflected in the world of manifestation. This might appear as a paradox, but that is precisely what the truth of the matter is. For example, you have empty rooms in Far Eastern art or Islamic art. These civilizations emphasized so much the significance of emptiness in art, or let us say more specifically, emptiness in a Chinese landscape painting, which is nothing, is emptiness, and then you have little mountains and even smaller men walking on a bridge or something like that. This element is very important in creating a kind of calm emptiness and peace externally reflecting that contemplative silence that is inward. The effect such art has upon the environment around it is precisely to allow in a sense the sacred forms of sacred art "to breath" and not to become stifled, suffocated by forms and excluded from the void and emptiness, from this openness unto the Infinite.

EL-ZEIN: When we look at beautiful works of calligraphy illustrating the verses of the Qur'an with letters in different undulations and shapes, we have the feeling that the letters are beings displaying powers of their own. We know that throughout Islamic countries, the Arabic letters were and are still used as a kind of talisman or symbol to protect from evil. Also, when we listen to the *tajwid* (Qur'anic recitation), we feel that the letters chanted display similar powers. Which, in your opinion, is closer to the truth of the Qur'an, the *haqiqah qur'aniyyah*, the sonoral art of *tajwid*, or the visual art of calligraphy?

Nasr: This is a very good question. The base, the foundation is, of course, the sonoral Revelation. The Qur'an was before anything else a sonoral revelation before being written down, a truth to which some scholars do not pay much attention these days. So, I would say that the highest form of sacred art in Islam is the recitation of the Qur'an, which the Prophet heard originally from the archangel Gabriel, hearing not only the words, but also the art of expressing the words. Since these various schools of *tajwid* (Qur'anic recitation) and *qira'ah* (readings) and other arts of Qur'anic recitation go back to the origin of Islam, I would say that the sonoral art is the central Islamic art. But since we not only have ears but also eyes, and these are the two most important of the five senses with which art deals, the recitation and calligraphy of the Qur'an are the highest forms of Islamic art along with sacred architecture which creates the space for the recitation of God's word. Of course, there are also arts associated with tasting, smell, and touch, but it is really seeing and hearing that are the most important when it comes to the revelation of God's sacred scripture and the arts related to it. The Qur'an keeps repeating that God is the All-Hearing, the All-Seeing, *Allahu al-sami'*, *al-basir*. These two Qualities of God are mentioned together. The power of vision complements that of hearing. Therefore, the importance of the written word, the calligraphy, the actual writing, complements the sonoral word, which, however, comes first both historically and metaphysically. In the traditional Islamic world, small children are first taught to recite certain Qur'anic formulas, even before they are taught the alphabet. There is no Muslim whose soul is not attuned to the hearing of the Qur'an, and the sonoral art is even more ubiquitous than the written art as far as the Qur'an is concerned.

EL-ZEIN: Arabic letters also have their own preeminence. Ibn 'Arabi, in *al-Futuhat al-makkiyyah*, devotes a whole chapter in which he considers them "beings" and unveils their different powers. If we consider them beings, what is then their relation as beings to artistic forms in Islam?

NASR: Each letter of the Arabic alphabet, the sacred language of the Qur'an, such as *nun*, *aliph*, *waw*, *ba'*, et cetera, are not only signs to be put together to create a word, for example, *baba* to signify "father." Of course, they do perform that function, but, much more than that, each single letter is like an emanation of Divine Power and Knowledge, because through them the Word of God is manifested. They are in reality beings and not just signs on a piece of paper, where you just draw a vertical line and say this is *aliph*; you draw a horizontal line with a dot underneath, and you say this is *ba'*. Individual letters are so but not only so. For example, *aliph* appears within a word, such as the Divine Name "Allah," which as a whole is sacred, but the *aliph* by itself is also a "being" with sacred meaning.

Now, that reality is related to Islamic art in the following way: the way that each letter is written, like, let us say, writing an *aliph* is not unique; there are different ways of writing it, directly or with a certain curvature, and so forth. And these variations are really different forms of possibilities, artistic possibilities to write that letter and have a relation to the "being" of that letter as a reality unto itself. For example, let us take the letter *nun*, which is a semicircle with a dot in the middle of it, that of course has many symbolic meanings. It is like the ship of creation with the dot contained inside the ship. It symbolizes manifestation and all the possibilities of Divine creation. Then we have the Qur'anic verse, *nun wa'l-qalam*, and so the *nun* is like the inkpot in which you put the *qalam* (pen) to write things. And, therefore, it is the symbol of all manifestation.

The very form of the letter *nun* not only looks like a ship, but also corresponds to that reality which the letter *nun* symbolizes and the very form in which it is written brings to mind that inkpot containing the ink used by the Divine Pen to create the whole manifested order. This is a very subtle matter. The letters of the Arabic alphabet have almost an esoteric meaning and a charismatic power that they can wield, but I will not go into that matter here. It is also important to note the way that these letters used in the art of calligraphy are envisaged, the impact that they have on the soul, not only when they are written on a piece of paper but also in mosques, in architecture where you often see various letters written which are "personalities," "beings" in themselves in addition to playing a role in the creation of words.

EL-ZEIN: You coined the expression "Abrahamic Pythagoreanism." How can Pythagoras be Abrahamic? What is the relation between both? Can you elucidate on this?

NASR: First of all, this term was coined by Frithjof Schuon and not by me. Yes, Pythagoras, of course, was a famous Greek philosopher of the sixth century BCE. And when we talk within the context of the Western and Islamic traditions, we identify this particular philosophy, which sees mathematics as the principle of things and associates numbers and geometric figures with spiritual entities, in a sense with Platonism and the Platonic ideas. When we say Pythagorean philosophy of mathematics, we mean the qualitative metaphysical understanding of mathematics. Now, Pythagoras was not, of course, a follower of the Abrahamic faith, but his ideas found a home in the Abrahamic world. But it was not only through the influence of Pythagoras that mathematics became so pertinent in Islamic art as a spiritual vehicle, as having qualitative significance. In this matter one must consider also the structure of Islamic Revelation itself. It is both these elements combined that Schuon and I call "Abrahamic Pythagoreanism."

You can also speak of Abrahamic Pythagoreanism to a lesser extent in Judaism with the symbolism of the letters of the Hebrew alphabet in the Kabbala, although in Judaism we do not have as much of an artistic manifestation of this doctrine in the world of architecture and calligraphy as we have in Islam. Still, it had its effect on certain commentaries upon the Torah and on Jewish art. But since Jewish architecture is not as prevalent as Islamic architecture, you cannot give examples so easily in this field. Nevertheless, some influence of its teachings did exist there. In Christianity, interestingly enough, Pythagoreanism always had trouble finding a home for itself intellectually, much more so than in the Islamic world, but we do see the prevalent influence of symbolic arithmetic and geometry related to Pythagorean philosophy in medieval Christian architecture.

EL-ZEIN: Why is that so?

NASR: Perhaps because in Christianity, with its doctrine of the Trinity, the aspect of Divine Unity was not as much emphasized as in Islam, and also because Christianity, its sapiential dimension, was mostly a way of love, whereas of course Pythagoreanism is an esoterism based upon knowledge. It is based upon *ma'rifah*, knowledge, and therefore it could find room for itself much more readily within Islam, not that it could not find at all a home for itself in Christianity. One cannot say that, because you could not have built medieval cathedrals without the integration of Pythagoreanism into the Christian perspective, but the mainstream Christian philosophy was much more wary of Pythagoreanism than the situation we have in Islam in which many embraced Pythagoreanism and even considered Pythagoras to have been a prophet.

Anyway, to come back to Abrahamic Pythagoreanism, it is important to understand that Pythagoras did not start everything from zero; he was deeply influenced by both Egyptian and ancient Persian teachings. We know that beyond any speck of doubt. And so, in a sense, we do not have just a sort of juxtaposition of Greek religion against Middle Eastern Abrahamic religion; that is not the case at all. Pythagoreanism itself is deeply "Oriental" in the way of its conceiving numbers and figures and of the philosophy that goes with mathematics. It is remarkable how in the Islamic context people felt so much at home with Pythagoras. One of the most important treatises of the Ikhwan al-Safa', which deals with Islamic Pythagorean teachings and the symbols of mathematics, says explicitly that he was among the people of unity; he was a *muwahhid*, a unitarian. They saw him as a person who asserted Divine Unity and even considered him to be a prophet.

EL-ZEIN: These symbols of mathematics of which you speak—are they not also very central in Islamic art?

NASR: Yes, they are. The central message of Islam is based on *ma'rifah* and the primacy of *'aql*, intellect or intelligence in its inner sense, which is considered to be a Divine gift to man. The structure of the Qu'ran, which itself, as I said, is not visible at first sight, is remarkable in its mathematical structure, numerical symbolism associated with *jafr*, symbols of letters and words, all of these elements combined together, most of all the emphasis upon unity (*tawhid*). All of these elements added together create an art, a sacred art, which is visibly more mathematical than any other sacred art in the world. Mind you, sacred art is based strictly on sacred geometry and arithmetic. For example, in the traditional images of the Buddha or a Christian icon, one sees outwardly a statue or a painting of a holy figure, but there are mathematical ratios and proportions in such work that are followed strictly. But in these forms of sacred art, the mathematical pattern is hidden. In much of Islamic art, however, it is the other way around. It is the mathematical form that is manifest and any other form is, one might say, secondary. So, you look at a mosque portal as you enter it; for example, a mosque from the Mamluk period or the Taymurid period. They display openly remarkable geometry. The main meaning is revealed in sacred geometry and you feel yourself to be in this world of mathematics in its archetypal reality, and you realize that all the little geometrical details have to do with the sacred. In contrast, today for many this type of understanding of what is involved seems to be incongruous, because the loss of understanding of mathematics as sacred in the modern worldview makes the understanding of the Islamic perspective difficult.

One cannot understand Islamic art without understanding the significance of the qualitative meaning of mathematics, of sacred geometry, and of the sacred quality of numbers. But Islamic art based on this sacred reality is created on the plane of material forms but as they reflect the intelligible world to the extent possible. For the Muslim mind, the world of intelligibility is represented directly by the mathematical world. Nowadays, many mathematicians and many theoretical physicists also assert that intelligibility in physics means mathematical formulas, mathematical descriptions of phenomena. But there is a big difference involved here. In this latter understanding of mathematics, there is no archetypal reality behind the mathematical forms. The mathematics itself is the ultimate form of intelligibility. But of course, in the Islamic context the mathematical forms themselves, whether they be geometrical forms or numbers, are themselves symbols of the purely archetypal formless world, where reality is not exhausted by nor does it depend on mathematical forms.

EL-ZEIN: In this sense, mathematics are symbols for metaphysics. And in this sense also, there is a need to resacralize mathematics.

NASR: Absolutely. It is not accidental that in the old days in the Islamic educational system people were taught mathematics before being taught metaphysics.

E-Zein: How do works of art affect our lives, whether we are surrounded by beautiful paintings or ugly ones? What is, in your opinion, the relation in art between being and seeing?

NASR: That is a very important relationship. On the one hand, the artist produces what he is, for the work of art is a reflection of the being of the artist. On the other hand, what is produced then affects the mode of one's being. There is a kind of cycle from A to B and then B to A. But it is not a vicious circle, because first of all you have point A, the soul of the artist. In traditional civilizations, there were principles and objective norms that the artist had to obey; the soul had to be disciplined. It had to submit itself to the Spirit, the spiritual realities, and then produce art under those conditions. In the modern world, all of those conditions have been removed, and so the soul of the artist usually produces something only on the basis of its subjective state even if it claims some form of objectivity. That soul could be chaotic, could be full of evil, could have fissures in it, could have all kinds of difficulties, all kinds of shortcomings, all kinds of dark elements; but the artistic creativity would be there irrespective of whether the artist has purified his own being or not.

So a work is produced which then others see. Now, to see or experience a work of art, which is the product of a soul that is chaotic, that is impregnated with the inferior human elements within us, what theologians would call the demonic or the satanic, to behold such a work is to also be affected by it. So then, we go from B, not back to A, which is the soul of the artist, but to an A1, which is the soul of the beholder of the work that is produced by the agent A. So, you go from the soul of the artist A to the work of art that he has produced B, and then by seeing that B, another soul A1 is affected by it. Surely, the impression upon our soul by what surrounds us is not neutral. It could be positive; it could be negative. It is hardly ever neutral.

One of the great tragedies of today's world is that so many people take ugliness for granted and gradually become numb to it. As a result, their soul "shrivels," spiritually speaking. If they see beauty, they say, "Oh, but that is luxury; I should not go after it and seek beauty and the beautiful at all possible levels." Most human beings are trained in the modern world to always look at the underbelly of everything, to try to find its ugly element and say, "Ah, this is what is real." Beauty becomes secondary. Actually, in the world of creation it is beauty that is real, and ugliness is transient, evanescent, and secondary. But we have become paralyzed by the modern situation and lost our sense of discernment both intellectually and artistically. That is why there is so much ugliness that surrounds us. And the reason we accept it is because we have now become insensitive; we have become affected to the extent of taking ugliness to be the norm. If you were to take completely traditional people, whether they would be Balinese or Muslims from Afghanistan or from faraway places or let us say Native American Indians, and show them modern art, I do not mean by modern art only post-Picasso but the post-traditional art of the West, it would be a horrendous experience for them. We have, in fact, records of that phenomenon. When these Rococo and Baroque churches were built by the Spaniards in South America and some of the Native Americans were brought into those churches, it was a horrifying experience for them. Whereas for the Europeans, they had gotten used to it and therefore they did not rebel against it. This is a fact that so many ugly works, which are called art today, are around us and there is no protest against it by most people. This is the proof of how seeing affects being and also how our being affects how we see things and evaluate them.

EL-ZEIN: And how do you relate this to God being the supreme artist?

NASR: We are made in the "image of God," and because God is the Supreme Artist, we can create art. But God has also given us the freedom of deviation and perversion, so that we can create things which deny God and the spiritual world. God being the Supreme Artist means that, first of all, everything He has created bears the imprint of His art, such as the world of nature and the soul of man. But in the case of man, as I said, He has not only made us in His image, but He has also given us the freedom to rebel against Him. So, we share, of course in a limited manner, in God's creative Power. If God were not the Supreme Artist, there would be no art. But that does not mean that automatically all the art that human beings have produced is Divine Art, or sacred art, precisely because of this element of freedom of human will and our ontological separation from God. But the great works of sacred art, which men have produced, in a sense are echoes of the Divine Art. Creation itself as well as traditional art, especially its sacred core, prove that God is the Supreme Artist.

EL-ZEIN: These "echoes of divine art," as you say, span in Islam a wonderful variety, from Persia to India to the Arab world. I want to specifically focus on Persia and the Arab world; how do you view the differences between Arabic Islamic art and Persian Islamic art? I am especially thinking of the Persian miniature that emanates light and seems to be inspired by the *ishraqi* school of Suhrawardi.

NASR: The difference between Arabic Islamic art and Persian Islamic art is not essential, but there is a difference in certain manifestations of Islamic art between these two ethnic groups. The Arabs are Semites, and when Islam came upon the scene, it spiritualized, in a sense, the Semitic mentality, like Judaism, that also comes from a Semitic background and which like Islam emphasized the banishing and forbidding of iconic images. Among the Semites, there has always been a danger of making a mistake between the symbol and an idol, and all the Semitic religions, which created, you might say, iconic forms of art, died from idolatry, such as the ancient religions of Mesopotamia. And the fact that Christianity did not do so is because Christianity, in contrast to Judaism and Islam, moved spiritually and psychologically to a large extent out of the Semitic world into the non-Semitic Indo-European world, and also because Christianity emphasized the manifestation of God in the Son, whose image thus became central to its sacred art. Moreover, in a sense, Christ was Europeanized. Christianity went on to dominate the Aryan world of Europe, and therefore icons were allowed.

Now, the one big difference between Persian and Arabic Islamic art is in the field of the representation of images in art, precisely because of the psychological difference between the Arabs or Semites and the Persians who were Indo-Iranians. On the highest level, there is unity in Islamic art. That is why it is forbidden that God be represented as an icon in Persian Islamic art as much as Arabic Islamic art. There is no doubt about that fact. Therefore, much of what is central to Islamic art is shared between the two: centrality of the importance of the void, geometric patterns, rhythms, all of these things which characterize Islamic art as a whole, whether it be Moroccan, Egyptian, Persian, Syrian, or otherwise. There is, however, this possibility open within the world of Islamic art for Persians of the creating of images but not in a way that it would be iconic, and images always remained on a small scale as the term miniature implies, in order not to humanize the Divine, and also because Islam is so much against anthropomorphism and also naturalism, both of which are also very important for Islamic spiritual principles. So, the Arabs, except perhaps for the Baghdad school of art, which was in any case close to the Persian world, did not produce figurative art except for folk art, while among the Persians figurative art became much more developed and Persia and to a lesser extent Turkey and Muslim India produced some of the greatest works of painting for a long time. But this tradition always remained faithful to the major principles of Islamic art. Moreover, sculpture was excluded from Islamic art everywhere.

EL-ZEIN: What distinguishes the Persian miniature?

NASR: First of all, the avoidance of the representation of the Divinity, not being an icon in the Christian sense. The miniature does not perform the same religious function at all. We do not put it in a mosque, *astaghfiru'Llah* (God forbid), and of course we do not find a mosque in Iran with miniatures for decoration. Secondly, the Persian miniature avoids the danger of naturalism, which the West faced at the end of the Middle Ages and which helped to destroy traditional Christian art as gradually forms became more and more naturalistic. The miniature adopted another style of painting, which was always two-dimensional and did not seek to create the illusion of three dimensions on a two-dimensional surface. It created a certain depiction of space that evokes the imaginal world that transcends this world. The colors of miniatures are also not naturalistic with pink mountains and so forth.

There is also the tradition of *Ishraq*, of illumination founded by Suhrawardi, which is so important in later Persian thought and which also spread into Syria, Turkey, and certain other places, but its center remained Persia, where light had always played such an important role going back to the ancient Iranian religion of Mazdaism. This use of light was brought into the Persian miniature, and therefore you do get, as you said quite rightly, light emanating from within these forms, and it is a very successful mode of creating art, which is pictorial but not worldly and at the same time not iconic. It is not like a Hindu painting of a god or a Christian painting of Christ and does not perform that function. Yet, at the same time, it is a spiritual art even when it deals with epic subjects as in the *Shah-namah, The Book of Kings*, of Firdawsi, which is the national Persian epic almost, and which is also the most often illustrated work in all of Persian literature. But, of course, the *Shah-namah* is much more than the history of a people. It is like Homer, with a lot of mythology and mythic historical realities presented therein. But even when you have the scene of Rustam, the hero, doing something, there is a spiritual quality about it, because it involves a traditional form of art and its illustrations remain deeply faithful to the Islamic principles of art.

EL-ZEIN: We cannot talk about Islamic art without mentioning the *Ka'bah* as a major Islamic symbol. Could you speak about the centrality of the *Ka'bah* in Islamic art, especially in Islamic architecture?

NASR: Yes, the *Ka'bah* is the protoarchitecture of sacred Islamic architecture. In its total reality it is both architecture and beyond architecture. Of course, it is a building, but because of its remarkable function and simplicity, it is also an archetypal sacred form in pure geometry. It contains within itself, as I often say, following Titus Burckhardt, the principles of Islamic architecture. It is not a mosque—it does not have a minaret, for example—but first of all it is the center of "Islamic space," orienting men and women who live in that "space" to the center, where the heavenly axis meets the earth, and secondly, it reveals the significance of geometry in Islamic art and architecture. The symbolism of its dimensions and harmonic ratios, into which I cannot go now, are very significant. The sides of the *Ka'bah* are based on harmonic ratios which correspond to musical notes, a reality that is fundamental for the development of Islamic architecture. The key, in a sense, for the harmonics of Islamic architecture is found in the *Ka'bah*. And there are also many other elements, such as the qualities of stability and centrality. The *Ka'bah* represents the supreme center of the Islamic world. As such, it is "present" in all Islamic architecture and city planning. The traditional Islamic city was and remains oriented toward the *Ka'bah*. So, in a sense, the presence of the *Ka'bah* determines the quality of space of Islamic architecture and city planning, of the sacred architecture and by extension of the vernacular. The idea of a center and direction of the *qiblah* (the direction toward the *Ka'bah*) is essential to the religious life of Islam and Islamic architecture.

EL-ZEIN: How about its emptiness?

NASR: Yes, I am coming to that question, but the next point that I wish to mention concerns stability. The *Ka'bah* represents perfect stability among all the three-dimensional polygonal forms. The cube is the one that is most stable of these forms, and, as I mentioned, it is the prototypic reality of Islamic architecture, an architecture that creates stability. When you go to a great mosque, you feel the stable space, a sense of stability, and a peace that is based on stability. It is not like, let us say, a church where you experience a flowing and vertical movement and a sense of being pulled upward. In the traditional mosque, you have everything being stable and space resting upon itself. That is what the *Ka'bah* represents in its principial form.

Then, as you mentioned yourself, there is the question of emptiness. The *Ka'bah* is a center, which is also in a sense above and beyond ordinary form. So, it is the form of the formless, you might say, but at its center and heart there is emptiness, and this emptiness or void is absolutely crucial for the understanding of Islamic art. I have already written about this matter and Burckhardt wrote as well in a most brilliant fashion about this matter, the question of the void in Islamic art and its decoration including the arabesque. The space of the mosque is characterized by its emptiness, and the Divine Presence, or *hudur*, is associated with this emptiness. Moreover, the traditional Muslim home is never cluttered with furniture. It is always simple, and it is mostly empty. I can hardly overemphasize for you the significance of emptiness in all aspects of Islamic art. Then of course not only do you have the space itself, but you also have the arabesque and geometric forms, and when you go into an Islamic monument, even if it is Alhambra, which is a palace and not a mosque, you feel this spiritual emptiness as if the weight of matter is being lifted from you as you experience in a sense an *inshirah* (expansion), which frees you from the weight of materiality. The void is very significant from that point of view.

EL-ZEIN: Does not this emptiness make the Islamic tradition close to the Buddhist tradition, in a sense?

NASR: That element of it, yes. There is the significance of *shunyata*, the void, in Buddhism, which is very close to the Islamic metaphysical understanding of the void impregnated by the Divine Presence. But there is, of course, a difference also because Islam sees God as the person whom we address and Buddhism does not speak about that aspect of God, although later on Mahayana Buddhism did develop that aspect in its own way, but there is this element, yes, which the two share together even if Islamic sacred art is aniconic and Buddhist art iconic.

EL-ZEIN: This reminds me of Toshihiko Izutsu's wonderful book in which he makes a comparison between Taoism and Ibn 'Arabi. So, does Taoism also share this emptiness with Islam?

NASR: Yes, it does. You can see this reality especially in Taoist paintings, such as the great paintings of the Sung dynasty, in which most of the scroll is empty, and human beings and their creations, such as a bridge or a house, are depicted just at the bottom as small forms. It is the emptiness that dominates. So, the Muslim who has gained familiarity with such art will feel at home looking at such works.

EL-ZEIN: You often stress that there is an inner nexus between Islamic architecture and Islamic cosmology and angelology. Can you first expand on this relation between Islamic architecture and Islamic cosmology and angelology, and, second, can you elucidate why it is so crucial to keep this nexus between architecture and cosmology?

NASR: Yes, let me begin by saying that angelology is related to cosmology in nearly all traditions. I do not mean modern physical cosmology, but traditional cosmology taken in the universal sense as the science of the cosmos that encompasses all the levels of reality below God and therefore includes the angelic world. Angelology is in fact inseparable from cosmology. That point must be made very clear. In some religions, like those of India, you do not talk so much about angels as you talk about the gods. But the gods in the Indian world are really angels in the Abrahamic world. In the Zoroastrian world, there is much emphasis upon the angels as well. In Buddhism we talk about the buddhas, in Shintoism about the *kamis*, the spirits, but in all these cases you have a universe which is not limited to the physical and the psychological. There is always a spiritual universe, which we also call the angelic world, a dimension of cosmic reality that also has its own levels of existence.

Now, coming back to cosmology, it is impossible to create sacred architecture without having sacred cosmology, because sacred architecture is based upon cosmological principles, which relate a particular edifice to a reality beyond the merely human world and open it to the Divine Presence. Since between us and God there is also the cosmos, sacred architecture has a cosmic dimension. The columns of stone or brick, the space, the ceiling, and so forth, are also part of the cosmos, and so the correspondences between the architecture and the cosmos must be preserved and revealed. There is also a correspondence between the human being and the cosmos, between *al-insan al-kabir* and *al-insan al-saghir*, as we say in Arabic. Sacred architecture must bring out this correspondence so that human beings within the sacred edifice feel themselves to be related to and in harmony with the cosmos, while the cosmic reality serves as a ladder for a journey to God.

I would like to repeat here this wonderful sentence of Schuon who said, "When you are standing before a medieval cathedral you feel at the center of the universe. When you stand before a rococo or a baroque modern church you merely feel that you are in Europe." That is really the heart of it. Why is that? Because a medieval cathedral was based on sacred architecture, on the cosmology of Christianity; the same is true for a mosque, a Buddhist temple, or a Hindu temple, where you feel to be at the center of the universe because this edifice is not just based on the human fancy of some individual. It is based upon principles which relate it to the cosmos; so, in beholding it you feel to be at the center of the cosmos. Man by nature is the central being on earth. God has created us as such. That is why man is the vicegerent of God on earth. Hence, we must create edifices which reflect this central reality. I am very critical of many modernized Muslims who do not understand that truth because they are influenced by modern science, which rejected all traditional cosmologies. As a result, they cannot create fresh sacred architecture anymore.

There are all these modern mosques in Pakistan, Malaysia, Indonesia, some in Iran and elsewhere, mosques that are no longer traditional. I have in mind especially the big mosques, like the national mosque in Jakarta, which is one of the ugliest buildings that I have seen in my life. Moreover, it is in a country of two hundred million religious Muslims, a country 90 percent of whose people are Muslim. These are horrendous, a travesty against God, in a certain sense, made by people who are on a certain level innocent because they are ignorant of what is really involved. They think it does not matter what style or materials they use, as long as they are building a mosque, which is just a space for prayer. But how the mosque is built matters a great deal. In fact, there is nothing more important, artistically speaking, for Muslims than to preserve their traditional architecture. If modernized Muslims say, "Oh, but the Seljuqs built in the Seljuq style and the Ottomans in the Ottoman style and the Mamluks in the Mamluk style, et cetera, so why can we not build in twenty-first-century style?" They are uttering nonsensical arguments, the answer to which is that Seljuqs, Mamluks, and Ottomans were living within a world in which traditional cosmology and art were alive. Master builders knew and taught their principles and they were able to then apply them to the world of stone, brick, or mud, whereas most people today are no longer in that world. They have no knowledge of that traditional cosmology. What audacity they have to destroy the traditional architecture of their country to build something of the twenty-first century unrelated to their tradition. What in fact is the twenty-first century? What is the significance of the twenty-first century that separates us in a positive way from centuries gone by as far as spiritual principles are concerned? Nothing. Authentic architecture has to deal with truth. Of course, it has to take into consideration contingent elements, such as economic factors, social factors, demographic factors, pragmatic factors. Of course, nobody doubts that, but the principles remain immutable.

I am very glad that, for example, in Egypt, although it is not economically well-off like many other countries, the government forbids the building of modernistic mosques, and there are a number of traditional plans that architects can use. They are not all identical. Interestingly enough, in Egypt you find the ugliest apartment houses in Cairo—as ugly as the mosques are beautiful.

If we are going to continue to have Islamic architecture, we must continue to have Islamic cosmology. Piety is very important and essential, but that is not enough. You need knowledge. You cannot build a mosque with piety alone. That is a necessary but not sufficient cause. As Muslims we need to come back to the traditional sciences, in which the elements of nature, various forces, various directions, dimensions, and spaces were and are still used in such a way as to accord with what I said earlier; that is, a relationship with the Islamic cosmos in which man functions as the vicegerent of God on earth.

EL-ZEIN: We lost the meaning and the power of symbols. Native Americans and other traditions in the past believed that the art form had its own power and did not distinguish between the art form and its message or power. Would you agree that the situation we are in is due to our misunderstanding of what a symbol is?

NASR: In a sense, yes. In the deepest sense, everything created by God is a symbol. There are certain symbols in which there is a concentration of power that represents a direct correspondence between a particular form and a transcendent reality, which that form symbolizes. The power of traditional art comes from this reality. Now, all Islamic art is in that sense symbolic. The geometry, the arabesque, the various styles of plant forms, and so forth, all symbolize a reality. They are doors that open unto worlds beyond themselves. With traditional painting, it is also the same. The classical miniatures, for example, have a symbolic quality to them. And that is why they are also so closely related to the mystical texts about which you spoke. In poetry, your own field, symbolism is ubiquitous. Symbolism pervades everything. As for Native Americans, the primal people, and the aboriginals who still follow the primal religions, there is a vivid awareness of symbols pointing to and in fact being, in the deepest sense, the symbolized. The conceptual difference between the symbol and the symbolized that we usually make is not made by these people, for they do not have the need for it. They see things not only as things but as symbols, symbols in which the symbolized is powerfully present. They still live in a world in which the symbolist spirit is fully present.

EL-ZEIN: Modern man cannot comprehend how and why the symbol and the symbolized are one like the Native American.

NASR: Yes. In general, you have three levels: first of all, for ordinary people, they experience things as only facts. Second, the spiritual person sees in these things symbols of a reality beyond these things. Third, in the deepest sense, the symbol and the symbolized become one, as you mentioned. The primal peoples have kept something of the spirit to which I just referred as the symbolist spirit to which Schuon has referred before me in his writings, a spirit that modern man has lost, in the same manner that one could lose the sense of color and become color blind. Modern man cannot see natural objects as symbols nor create symbolic art in an authentic sense, but traditional man can. These archaic primal civilizations have a very strong sense of the symbolist spirit. And, therefore, they see in creatures not only a kind of abstract symbol or symbolized; they see what we call the symbolized directly in the symbol and the art that they create is symbolic. When they see an eagle fly, they say, "Ah, this is the spirit," and so they have been accused of pantheism. Now, in the later phase of human history, because of the gradual fall of men's perception of things, it was necessary for the religions, in order to prevent the idolatry of external forms, to come up with a clear distinction: spiritual realities transcend physical realities; God is the Absolute Transcendent Reality, but in sacred art they always had to bring the manifestation of that Reality back to the world of forms. Immanence had to be also ever present. Mystics especially were those who had been given the task of speaking about the immanent aspect of the Real and proximity of that Reality which is in itself transcendent.

In Islam a thousand years ago, theologians and philosophers debated about that issue, about the relation between *tashbih* (immanence) and *tanzih* (transcendence). The truth is that both are correct. In a sense, *tanzih* can be understood as transcendent, that which is beyond *tashbih*. *Tanzih* in its inner sense can be said to deal with symbols of *tashbih* to show that the symbol is not fact, that its reality transcends the merely factual. So, there is a very central and important issue involved here. To understand any traditional and especially sacred art, we must understand the language of symbolism.

EL-ZEIN: What do you say to those who have always criticized Islam for lacking symbolism?

NASR: I have heard that many times. This is, of course, totally false. Those who make such assertions are not really aware of what a symbol is. A symbol is that which unites a lower reality with a higher reality of which the lower is a manifestation and reflection. The Qur'an says, *bi-yadihi malakut kulli shay'* (in His Hand is Dominion—or dominating principle—over everything). To understand that verse in depth, one has to understand that *malakut* is that reality of which a *shay'* or thing is the symbol, that reality that determines the nature of a *shay'* and makes it be what it is.

Chapter 6

Sufism and Modernity

El-Zein: How does your own criticism of modernity continue that of Guénon and Schuon, and how does it differ from them?

Nasr: I have read numerous works of Coomaraswamy, which were collected under the title *The Bugbear of Literacy*, and later on, of course, all the books of Guénon and Schuon, whose criticism of the modern world was so fecund, so profound, and which influenced me deeply. I also studied the history of Western science, Western philosophy, Western thought, very extensively while studying at MIT and Harvard, and have also attended many courses even outside of my field of specialization. Therefore, I did not come to this discussion empty-handed. I would say that my own criticism of the modern world differs from the early masters of traditional thought in that it applies the same principles but to certain domains with which they did not deal. For example, my study of the crisis of the environment and what brought it about; neither Guénon nor Schuon paid much attention to this issue, but this does not mean that the principles that they expressed could not be applied to this matter. On the contrary, it is those very principles that served as an intellectual foundation for my criticism of modern man's relation to nature. The principles they expounded are the same as mine; for example, I have written very extensive critiques of modern science in relation to religion and in this discussion I always come back to the underlying Cartesian dualism or bifurcation, which is the foundation of modern science and which even quantum mechanics cannot get rid of, as I mentioned to you before. Therefore, it needs to be stated that in discussing principles I go back to the truths already stated by Coomaraswamy, Guénon, and Schuon, while I have applied them at times to domains with which they did not concern themselves.

There was much to learn on the level of facts as I was studying the history of science in the 1950s, and especially the crucial events in the rise of modernism, which is associated with the Renaissance and the Scientific Revolution. But even at that time, the foundation of my worldview was already that of the traditionalists. I had learned in detail how this transformation of the modern Western worldview came about through the eyes and the ears, you might say, of the famous philosopher of science Alexandre Koyré, through listening to his lectures and, of course, reading his books as well as those of Giorgio De Santillana and other profound scholars who dealt with this issue at that time. But I did so from the perspective of the principial and fundamental critiques that were being made by Guénon and Schuon and other traditional authorities. Hence my own criticism of modernity and modernism is based on the traditional works as well as my own study of them. I use the term "modernism" as a particular philosophy, and I use it more than "modernity"; sometimes I use modernity when it needs to be used, but I think the term "modernism" conforms more to the deviated worldview and philosophy which Schuon, Guénon, Coomaraswamy, and others criticized so profoundly, especially what pertained to the domains of philosophy, psychology, and art. I applied such criticism to certain other domains, such as modernism in the Islamic world and environmental studies.

EL-ZEIN: In the face of this bleak role of modern positivist science, you plead for the return of sacred science and you even predict, like Toynbee, that people in the future would be more inclined to pursue other activities, such as theology, art, and philosophy. What makes you think this change could happen in the postmodern Western society?

NASR: The idea that is held generally today, seen so clearly in the way modern education is presented, is that science—in its modern sense—represents the fruit of a long and continuous struggle of mankind (especially those in the West) for a more authentic knowledge of nature and "enlightenment" and all of those kinds of similar ways of thinking which originated in the seventeenth century and the European Enlightenment and which are part and parcel of the modern worldview. Most people in the West associate civilization with science as if the two were the same. I remember that my own teacher at Harvard, George Sarton, who was perhaps the greatest historian of science in the English-speaking world during the last century, always used to say, "Hossein, I am worried because when you look at the history of science, you see that the great civilizations of the world, Islam being the only exception, produced outstanding exact sciences, such as astronomy, mathematics, and the like at the end of their historical existence when they were dying out. Look at Babylonia, look at Greece, and so on. So, this emphasis upon science may be the swan song of Western civilization itself." He used to speak about this matter often. Of course, today the majority of the Western intelligentsia does not look upon this issue in this manner. But, of course, there was the famous historian Arnold Toynbee, who predicted that in the twenty-first century the Western intelligentsia would turn away from science to other pursuits.

Now, we do not see that occurrence on the horizon right now, not because of the love of the majority of people for science itself, but because of their love of comfort, of money, of material things which the applications of modern science provide for them. The driving force is not really the love of science itself. Rather, science is "sold" on the basis of its providing profit for them, material gain, bodily health, and similar considerations. One is told that one should give money for the good of mankind and for peace, you know these slogans, but not for the sake of pure knowledge. Rarely would one give any money to a university for the attainment of pure knowledge rather than its "beneficial" application, neither the government nor companies. Which industrial company would give any money to a place like MIT, RPI, or Stanford for the sake of pure knowledge? So, actually, today what is fanning this interest in modern science is power, wealth, and health. Modern science has been supported mostly for the sake of gaining power, power which until now was mostly military, political, and social, but now has turned more and more into technological power providing greater economic possibility and power, and "infinite" choices for a "consumer" society.

But at the same time this way of living is very rapidly leading to the destruction of the natural world, of the natural environment. So, already there are different reactions that we see concerning this pseudoreligion of modern science, one could call it, when in a world in which you want to sell something involving health on television, you bring a "person of knowledge of science," someone with a long white robe like that of a doctor or someone like that to sell the product. I believe that there are actually two movements against this total blind emulation and adulation of modern science, one of which comes as a result of the environmental crisis. There is a malaise in this domain that many feel and experience. Some would say, well, there is a solution to the environmental crisis, and that is more but wiser use of technology, more application of modern science, but many know deep down in their hearts that this is not so.

The second comes from an intellectual and spiritual search for what has been lost within the vacuum created by modernism, a search for what I call sacred science. That is the spiritual science of reality, including nature, the incomplete and truncated understanding of which has led today to all kinds of occultism, pseudoscience, and the New Age movement, which use some elements of traditional sciences such as astrology and alchemy and similar subjects and which the scientific enterprise finds very dangerous. Carl Sagan before he died was one of the priests of this kind of pseudoreligion of science and also spoke strongly against New Age tendencies. He wrote a popular book about that subject, but, nevertheless, both of these movements are still present. And if history continues, if we do not destroy ourselves with the applications of a materialistic science, it is quite possible that one would reach a state predicted by people such as Toynbee who claim that the main intellectual energy of Western civilization will turn to other pursuits than modern science.

El-Zein: Some authors argue, though, that we must have faith in human progress. I am thinking precisely of Carl Sagan, who you just mentioned, and especially of the last book he wrote before he died, *The Demon Haunted World: Science as a Candle in the Dark*. What are your thoughts on this work?

Nasr: I think it is like people singing in the dark, whistling in the dark, where they are afraid that they are going to be attacked any moment. I do not accept at all his thesis. Carl Sagan represents the people who want to have peace and happiness and harmony in the world without God, but God will never allow that. It is as simple as that.

El-Zein: In the face of the sweeping dangers of Western modernity, you often emphasize the impact of prayer on one's being, and you talk about the similarity between the

Christian Mass and the *salat*, the Muslim daily prayers. Can you first elucidate how the Christian Mass resembles the *salat*? And, second, how does the prayer help in regaining one's center in a Western world often devoid of soul?

NASR: As far as the Mass is concerned, when I talk about it, I mean the traditional form. The traditional Mass, whether Latin or Orthodox, is a rite which descended from Heaven; it is the emulation of the last supper of Christ and is a real celebration, which goes back to a reality beyond the individual, to the metahuman, in the same way the daily prayers, taught to the Prophet by the archangel Gabriel, take us beyond this world to the Divine Presence. These rites are not manmade; both of them are divine forms imposed upon a human collectivity. Therefore, they are not to be confused with individual prayer. In Islam, we have the *du'a'*, which is an individual supplication to God and which is very important, but it does not take the place of the *salat*, and the Christians also have individual prayers which they perform before going to bed, before meals, and so forth, and likewise the Christian individual prayers do not take the place of the Mass. Both the Mass and *salat* are divine rites imposed from Heaven upon the individual.

Another point which is very important to mention is that the Mass requires the presence of a priest and has certain rules and regulations; you cannot just do whatever you like. The same is true of the *salat*, with the difference that the priestly function in Islam is divided among all Muslims. As a man or woman, you can stand in front of God and pray according to a revealed form; when you perform the *salat*, you are fulfilling the function of a priest. Likewise, in the Mass there is always this priestly function that is involved, except that this function is limited to a particular class of believers and is not shared by everyone.

As to the question of one regaining one's center, first of all, let me say that one of the ways to understand what has happened in the modern world is precisely to go back to this question of the symbolism of the center. Schuon wrote a profound book entitled *To Have a Center* in which he discusses this point and also talks about modern man's frantic attempt to create a world without having a center. And Hans Meyer, the famous German art historian, once wrote a book in German called *Art without a Center* in which he tried to show Renaissance and post-Renaissance art of the West as an art that does not emanate from the center of man's being and therefore itself lacks a center.

Now, the *salat*, which connects us with God, must be connected to the center of our being. When we stand before God, we must be present at the center of our consciousness. The same thing holds true for the Mass. But if you are in Siberia, there might be no place to celebrate the Mass, whereas you can always say your *salat* anywhere you are. And that place where you perform your prayer becomes itself a center corresponding to the Holy of Holies in the Christian Church, which also represents the center. In the deepest sense, we carry our center within us whether we are Christian or Muslim, and the comparison between the two religions should be made with that reality in mind.

EL-ZEIN: Since we are talking about Islamic prayer and Christian Mass, I would like to continue the dialogue along the lines of Christianity and Islam, but this time with regard to exegesis. In *The Need for a Sacred Science*, you criticize what you call "the theological modernism" of Hans Küng, because you think that it kills the inner meaning of the sacred texts and closes the door to the spiritual world. What is in your opinion the difference between the theological modernism of someone like Kung and that of Qur'anic medieval exegesis, *ta'wil*?

NASR: The difference is very plain. In fact, Christianity in the Middle Ages also had something like *ta'wil* that most modern Christian theologians, even Kung, overlook. Remember that Dante speaks of the four levels of meaning of both sacred scriptures and his own *Divine Comedy*, from the literal, to the moral, to the analogical, to the anagogical, which is the purely symbolic and spiritual significance of a text. Higher criticism should mean to reach the higher, and the more inward, meaning of a sacred text or any inspired text. There is a metaphysics that underlies traditional epistemology associated with a critical study of it. You had levels of reality and levels of knowledge according to medieval Christianity, as we have in the Qur'an. We have the external meaning of the Qur'an, and then the various levels of inner meanings. There is a famous *hadith* of the Prophet that can be summarized as saying that there are seven levels of meaning to the Qur'an of which the seventh is known only by God. You have the levels of reality of the Qur'an as it descends from the Divine Reality to our world, and you have levels of understanding of the Qur'an. And this is true mutatis mutandis of other sacred scriptures. As I said, Dante speaks about levels of meaning, and it is certainly not unique to Islam.

However, what is called "higher criticism" these days is an inversion of this whole metaphysical reality. This type of criticism arose in the nineteenth century when reality was reduced to historical process and the vision of immutability lost. What appears as "higher" in this perspective is actually a reduction to temporality, to change, and therefore the immutable and that which is transhistorical is reduced to the lower. It is the complete inversion of the traditional inner understanding of a sacred text. For example, we have the story of Abraham taking place in the Qur'an. Now, at a certain level it is history, but that is in fact the most external meaning. There are all kinds of higher meanings. The sacrifice of Abraham is also the sacrifice that the *nafs* has to perform before God and has many levels of meaning. To take the purely historical meaning is like saying that yes there was such a man having a long beard walking in a desert somewhere in the Middle East and that is the highest meaning of this account of sacred history. According to this perspective, only change is real, only the transient is real. So, "higher criticism," in this sense, means to try to find out the historical consistency of the Bible, distinguishing what "really happened" historically from myth and symbolic understanding of events of sacred history, to see if the various accounts match or not, which manuscript is older, which is more recent and less reliable, and so on. It is to try to reduce all that is real to what is historically verifiable, which means to deny the vertical transcendent dimension and to deny oral tradition. In this sense, you could say the whole apostolic succession does not exist, because we do not have a written document showing Christ handing the "key" of the church to Saint Peter. Nor do we have a document signed by him, or something like that. Searching always for physical clues, for physical manuscripts, for physical archeological evidence and then on the basis of these things trying to judge the sacred text is really the death of the spiritual significance of tradition and of a sacred text. It is one of the greatest shocks that Christianity received in the nineteenth century.

EL-ZEIN: Do you not think that Islam did not have this kind of "higher criticism" because there is only one sacred text?

NASR: That is right; Islam did not produce this kind of criticism as far as the text of the Qur'an is concerned, but the Orientalists for two hundred years have been nevertheless trying to do something similar for Islam as we see in the West in its pursuit of modern higher criticism. The mindset in much of Western religious scholarship is such that higher criticism is applied not only to the text of the Bible but also in a sense to the life of Christ. Christ's life and that he is the Word of God is also mentioned in the Qur'an. Some Western scholars of religion have even tried to analyze and refute this Qur'anic doctrine concerning him. So, gradually among modern Christians many begin to doubt his miraculous birth. How many Christians in the West now believe that the virgin was a virgin when she gave birth to Christ? Many interpret this assertion as being metaphorical, allegorical, and they destroy even the literal meaning of sacred texts. Once you destroy the literal meaning the higher meanings become impossible to reach.

EL-ZEIN: You also criticize Hans Küng for saying, "Theology should not be an esoteric science only for the believers but should be intelligible to non-believers as well." Is religion in postmodern Western society losing its esoterism? And is there not always a risk in esoterism to be restricted to the elite?

NASR: First of all, Western Christianity already lost access to most of its esoteric teachings several centuries ago. Moreover, that was, I believe, the main crisis in Western religion, which brought about the separation of philosophy, science, and several other disciplines from religion. One might ask, Why is it that the West had produced so many post-Christian atheists? Why do you not have this phenomenon on the same scale in Hinduism, Islam, and other religions? That is certainly a good question to ponder upon. Is that because Europeans are so intelligent that they became atheists and the rest of the world was stupid and remained bound to religion? Nobody will accept that view any more, although a modified version of it was propagated for a long time. We must look for some other cause, and I think the deeper cause is the restrictions placed upon esoterism gradually causing its suffocation in the West so it was no longer a main force. Some of it survived here and there; but it was not like in Islam, where you had the continuously living tradition of Sufism, or in Hinduism, where esoteric teachings thrived, or in Buddhism, where you had Zen and other forms of Japanese esoteric Buddhism, and so on. The loss of esoterism in the West had already taken place before our period and on a scale very different from elsewhere.

As for the second part of your question, it really needs to be answered very categorically, and that is that esoterism is by definition addressed to the few. If you want to call the few an elite, so be it. We call the elite *al-khawass* in Arabic, to oppose it to *al-ʿawam*, the general public, and it has a very positive connotation. In English, however, the word "elite" has gained a pejorative sense because of a false notion of democracy which claims that everyone is equal in every way. But I ask you this question: How many people in the city of Washington can understand the latest theories of quantum mechanics? Not more than a few hundred. It is knowledge accessible to a very small elite, but nobody criticizes that assertion. On another level how many people can understand the structure of a Brahms symphony? Very few, because of its incredible complex structure; the rest of us listen to it and nevertheless enjoy it. So, the assertion that the concept of an elite is negative is totally false. What makes civilization possible is having elites in various domains. How many students did Socrates and Plato have? Maybe ten or twenty, but they continued a whole philosophical tradition. Few people pay attention to that reality. And was not Einstein among the elite in physics? Of course he was. Was not Mozart also an elite musician? Yes, he certainly was. There was not even a small group that could compare to such elite composers as Mozart and Hayden during their generation.

When I speak of the authentic elite, I do not mean a financial class that has become very rich with exceptional privileges, dominating over others. In fact, the demonization of the word "elite" comes mostly from both Western democracy and Marxism, which based their criticism of it on political, social, and economic privilege not supported by one's own effort but mostly inherited. But, in reality, society cannot do without what is created by elites, from the philosophy and science of Plato and Aristotle to the poetry of Dante to the music of Bach. The gift provided by the elite percolates throughout the whole of society. Here is another example, this time from Islam. You just gave me an article that you wrote on Rumi. If there ever was an elite person, it was Rumi. He was an esoteric master of the highest order. Look at the emanation of his influence even now, 750 years after his death. People, even here in the United States, in Europe, in Persia, in Turkey, in Central Asia, in India, still read his poetry. And in the Arab world Ibn ʿArabi was another elite esoteric master. Look at his contribution to Arabic literature and Islamic spirituality. I have no problem with being called the person who defends elitism. Within every field there is an elite; for example, in mathematics today we have an elite group who really determine what mathematics today is and where it is going, what is acceptable as mathematics. You and I have no democratic voice to contribute to such matters. So, let us not worry about elitism in its authentic sense. Once again, I stress that the great tragedy in the West was that esoterism in its spiritual and religious sense was eclipsed, and one might add that the spiritual elite nearly disappeared. What remained was only the more external aspects of religion, which could not provide a response to the challenges that were made against it. And once responses to those responses were not available, many intelligent people in the West left Christianity.

EL-ZEIN: You often come to the idea that Hinduism and Islam know no distinction between the sacred and the secular and that they both envisage religion in its worldwide expressions throughout the cycles of human history. Can you explain how Hinduism and Islam are close to each other and how they can work together in the postmodern age?

NASR: First of all, despite a very few clashes here and there, the two religions succeeded to a large extent in living and working together in the past. We had several centuries of remarkable harmony between Hinduism and Islam in

India. However, the British colonization of India destroyed this equilibrium and led to the unfortunate situation we have today. It is true, though, that there were some Muslim movements in the past that expressed their fear that Islam might be absorbed into Hinduism and reacted against Hindu influences and, I might add, vice versa. These fears have intensified in both India and Pakistan today with the rise of both Hindu and Islamic fundamentalism in the subcontinent. In earlier times, when Muslims ruled over much of India at the other end of the spectrum, there were a number of rulers and many Sufi masters who in fact believed that there should be concord and accommodation between the two religions and the "meeting of two seas," as Dara Shukuh has said.

Today, one of the great tragedies, not only for India itself, but also for Pakistan and Bangladesh, is that those elements of harmony do not really have the voices that they should have. There are incredible possibilities of positive relationship between Hinduism and Islam. First of all, both encompass the whole of life. Hinduism is still very vibrant, like Islam. The Hindu temples are full of believers, like the Islamic mosque; there is a great deal of piety in both religions, unlike in much of the West, especially in Europe, where if you go in a church you will not find more than a few worshipers. In India you have a modernized class in Delhi and other big cities who have become secularized and modernized, as you have in Pakistani cities, but the vast majority of Hindus are still very devout, as are Muslims. There is a great deal of living religion and spirituality in India, like in the Islamic world. In both of these worlds there is still a ubiquitous presence and manifestation of religion, as we see in communal prayers, millions of pilgrims, and so forth. In today's world, such manifestations occurring on a wide basis are only to be seen in Islam and Hinduism. Secondly, both religions, as you mentioned in your question, refuse to separate the sacred and the profane or, one might say, the sacred and the secular. The whole of life is integrated for both into a single sacred reality, and the whole spectrum of life, from the outside to the inside, from the outward to the inward, everything has a sacred aspect to it. And then Hinduism, as a remnant of the primordial religion, has the vision of the various avatars manifesting themselves throughout the whole history of the present cosmic cycle. Therefore, it is not in principle exclusivist. Islam, coming from the Abrahamic world, coming at the tail end of human sacred history is also not exclusivist. It does not believe that any revelation will come after the Quranic, and there will not be another Divine intervention in human history until the end of the world and eschatological events connected with the figure of the Mahdi and Christ. Islam sees all the earlier prophets, or in Indian languages avatars, as belonging to the same spiritual world as its world. It accepts all the prophets before it, and therefore has not had any trouble, when it has met other authentic religions, to accommodate them; not only Christianity and Judaism, but also Zoroastrianism in Persia, Hinduism in India, Buddhism in Afghanistan and Eastern Iran, Shamanism in Central Asia, African religions, in fact, almost every religion near and far, even Taoism and Confucianism in China. Today, scholars are discovering all kinds of works of Chinese Muslims in which Confucius is considered to be a prophet, and Chinese Muslims saw Confucianism as one of those religions that Islam could accept to be of *ahl al-kitab*, People of the Book.

And so these two religions, Islam and Hinduism, although in many ways different, are at the same time in many other ways alike and complementary. Above all, they both have a very elaborate metaphysics and meet actually on the highest level intellectually and spiritually. That is why there were all of these works written in India comparing the doctrines of Ibn ʿArabi, such as *wahdat al-wujud*, with the nonduality principle of *Advaita Vedanta* as expounded by Shankara; there are, in fact, remarkable similarities between the two.

EL-ZEIN: Do you think that the notion of balance, the fact of putting everything in its due place, is behind this capacity of accommodation, as you say, that Islam has?

NASR: Yes, it is certainly an important notion, mentioned also in the Qur'an. Islam emphasizes both the importance of everyday life covered by religious principles and the spiritual life which transcends everyday life, and it avoids the extremes of hedonism and excessive asceticism. I know some Muslim writers have written about this matter, but often in a rather shallow way. There is a more profound dimension to it. Islam is profoundly realist; that is, it wants to put each thing that we see in the world of reality above us and within us in its proper place. It seeks to avoid exaggeration and going to extremes. However, this question of hedonism and asceticism is only one dimension of it. There is the injunction of not amassing too much wealth and not living in abject poverty, refusing to work, paying too much attention to one aspect of life, not paying attention to it at all, and so on. This balance (*al-mizan*) is always with the goal of preparing the soul properly for the other life, *al-akhirah*. The Qur'an mentions, "*al-akhirah khayrun laka min al-ula*" (the next life is better for you than this life). And there are some Muslim modernists who say that Islam balances this world with the next, but this world can never be balanced with the next, precisely because the next is so much more real. But even with this world of impermanence, one should still put each thing in its own place. One should live a life that is balanced but always in light of the remembrance of *al-akhirah* and the goal for which God has given us life in this world.

One of the very fundamental theses of the Qur'an is the brittleness of this world, its transience, its lack of permanence. In many *surahs* of the Qur'an, such as *surat al-waqi'ah*, it is so clearly stated that everything will ultimately fall apart and suffer death except God. There are very powerful images of this truth in the Qur'an that demonstrate vividly the lack of permanence of this world. The love for one's family, the neighbor, work, rest, nature, and art, all have their place in the life of the Muslim, but the love of God reigns supreme. Islam is having trouble in this modern urban setting in preserving that balance that Islam manifests, while the traditional Islamic life has always been based on a remarkably balanced view of life within a circle whose Center is God, the Center to which we shall all return. The *Ka'bah*, which is the supreme symbol of Islam, is a cube, the most stable of many-sided figures; it is the luminous symbol of stability itself, the stability that characterizes traditional Islamic society and the life of the traditional Muslim individual and the ground from which the highest flight of the bird of the spirit takes place to the Divine Empyrean.

Notes

Introduction

1. Seyyed Hossein Nasr, "Reply to Leonard Lewisohn," in *The Philosophy of Seyyed Hossein Nasr*, ed. Lewis Edwin Hahn, Randall E. Auxier, and Lucian W. Stone, Jr., Library of Living Philosophers 28 (Chicago: Open Court, 2001), 679.

2. Seyyed Hossein Nasr, *The Need for a Sacred Science* (Albany: State University of New York Press, 1993), 60. See also chapter 1 in the present volume.

3. Seyyed Hossein Nasr, "Reply to Ernest Wolf-Gazo," in *The Philosophy of Seyyed Hossein Nasr*, 308.

4. Seyyed Hossein Nasr, *An Introduction to Islamic Cosmological Doctrines: Conceptions of Nature and Methods Used for Its Study by the Ikhwān al-Ṣafā', al-Bīrūnī, and Ibn Sīnā* (Albany: State University of New York Press, 1993), 5.

5. Nasr, *The Need for a Sacred Science*, 87.

6. Seyyed Hossein Nasr, "The Contemporary Islamic World and the Environmental Crisis," *Sophia* 13, no. 2 (2007): 13–35.

7. Seyyed Hossein Nasr, *Religion and the Order of Nature* (Oxford: Oxford University Press, 1996), 5.

8. Seyyed Hossein Nasr, *Knowledge and the Sacred* (New York: Crossroad, 1981), 45.

9. Seyyed Hossein Nasr, "Contemporary Man between the Rim and the Axis," in *Science and the Myth of Progress*, ed. Mehrdad M. Zarandi (Bloomington, IN: World Wisdom, 2003), 106–7.

10. Nasr, "Contemporary Man," 96–101.

11. Seyyed Hossein Nasr, *Sufi Essays*, 2nd ed. (Albany: State University of New York Press, 1991), 154.

12. John (Fire) Lame Deer and Richard Erdoes, *Lame Deer, Seeker of Visions* (New York: Simon and Schuster, 1972), 265–66.

13. Ibn al-'Arabī, *Al-Futuhat al-Makkiyah* (Beirut: Dar Sader, n.d.), 2:456.

14. As quoted and translated by William Chittick in his book *The Sufi Path of Love: The Spiritual Teachings of Rumi* (Albany: State University of New York Press 1983), 159.

15. Seyyed Hossein Nasr, *Islamic Art and Spirituality* (Albany: State University of New York Press, 1987), 90.

16. Nassr, *Islamic Art and Spirituality*.

17. Nassr, *Islamic Art and Spirituality*, 129.

18. William C. Chittick, *The Self-Disclosure of God* (Albany: State University of New York Press, 1997), 77.

19. Ananda K. Coomaraswamy, *Figures of Speech or Figures of Thought? The Traditional View of Art* (Bloomington, IN: World Wisdom, 2007), 1.

20. Titus Burckhardt, *Mirror of the Intellect: Essays on Traditional Science and Sacred Art* (Albany: State University of New York Press, 1987), 117.

21. Seyyed Hossein Nasr, *Man and Nature: The Spiritual Crisis in Modern Man* (London: Unwin, 1990), 81.

22. Nasr, "Reply to Leonard Lewisohn," 681. See also the chapter he devotes to logic and poetry in in *Art and Spiritualty*, 87–97.

23. Huston Smith, *The Way Things Are: Conversations with Huston Smith on the Spiritual Life*, ed. Phil Cousineau (Berkeley: University of California Press, 2003), 193.

24. It is worth noting that traditionalism is an intellectual movement that was established in 1920 by the French thinker René Guenon; many important figures joined it, such as Frithjof Schuon, Julius Evola, and Mircea Eliade. By 2000, it became almost a famous movement that attracted other personalities, such as Nasr and Huston Smith, among others.

25. Nassr, *Knowledge and the Sacred*, 234.

26. Seyyed Hossein Nasr, *Islam in the Modern World: Challenged by the West, Threatened by Fundamentalism, Keeping Faith with Tradition* (New York: Harper One, 2010), 239.

Chapter 1

This dialogue was published as Seyyed Hossein Nasr and Amira El-Zein, "Sufism, Creativity and Exile," in "Culture, Creativity and Exile," ed. Issa J. Boullata and Husain Haddawy, special issue *Jusoor*, no. 7/8 (1996): 131–58.

    1. Seyyed Hossein Nasr, *Sufi Essays*, 2nd ed. (Albany: State University of New York Press, 1991), 37.

    2. Nasr, *Sufi Essays*, 37.

    3. Seyyed Hossein Nasr, *Présence de Louis Massignon* (Paris: Maisonneuve et Larose, 1987), 50.

Chapter 3

    1. Mircea Eliade, *Cosmos and History: The Myth of the Eternal Return* (New York: Harper, 1959).

Index

Abrahamic Pythagoreanism, 150–151, 175–176
Abu Bakr (companion), 156, 160
acupuncture, 108
Adam, Charles, 99
Adamic wisdom (*hikmah adamiyyah*), 46
al-'Adawiyyah, Rabi'ah, 40, 61
al-'alam al-saghir. See microcosm
al-alam-al-kabir. See macrocosm
al 'Alawi, Shaykh, 89, 140
alchemy, 129–130
Alchemy (Burckhardt), 130
Alfiyyah (Ibn-Malik), 138
Ali (Fourth caliph), 156–157
aliph (first letter of the Arabic alphabet), 174
ana. See I
ana'iyyah. See I-ness
angelic world (*jabarut*), 62
angelology, 23, 57–58, 186–187
annihilation (*fana'*), 43
anti-traditional civilization, the West as, 27
'aql. See intellect

Arab and Persian poets, Western poets emulated by, 30–31, 137
Arabic, al-Qummi writing in, 89
Arabic letters, 174
Arabs, Persians contrasted with, 181–182
arba'in. See forty
archangelic world (*jabarut*), 62
archetypes, 168–170
architecture, sacred, 88–89
  See also Islamic architecture
Aristotle, 152, 170
arithmetic, sacred art based in, 177
art
  cosmology compared with, 68–69
  the Divine evoked by, 14–15
  emptiness in, 172
  of expressing words, 173
  imaginal world in relation to, 65
  power of, 190
  in relation to being and seeing, 178

213

art *(continued)*
  sonoral, 14
  Sufism and, 13, 165–166
  ugliness and, 179–180
  See also Islamic art; sacred art; traditional art
Art without a Center (Meyer), 199
ascension (*mi'raj*), 38, 60
asceticism, 207
Asrar al-'ibadat. See *The Secrets of Worship*
atheists, the West producing, 202
Attar, Farid al-Din, 10
  herbs sold by, 35
  Ilahi-Namah by, 162
  on words, 153
Augustine (saint), 21
al-'awam. See general public

balance (*al-mizan*), 207–208
Bangladesh, 205
Baqli, Ruzbihan, 12, 147
al-barakah al-muhamadiyyah. See Muhammadan grace
barzakh, 63, 65
al-Bastami, Bayazid, 60, 158
bay'ah. See initiatic pact
beauty
  God authoring, 167–168
  Hafiz portraying, 135–136
  knowledge and, 13
  ugliness contrasted with, 179–180
  See also art
being (*al-wujud*), 14, 123
Being and Time (Heidegger), 122

beloved (*habib*), 161
Bezels of Wisdom (*Fusus al-hikam*) (Ibn 'Arabi), 46
bid'ah. See innovation
bodily accession (*al-mi'raj al-jismani*), 38
the body, dancing integrating, 39
Boehme, Jacob, 82, 111, 121
Boehr, Niels, 76
Bohm, David, 78
Breton, André, 29
British colonization, of India, 205
Buddhism, 186–187, 202
The Bugbear of Literacy (Coomaraswamy), 193
Burckhardt, Titus, 14, 53, 69, 127, 130

calligraphy, 171–173
Campbell, Joseph, Hinduism believed in by, 126–127
canonical prayer (*salat*), 86
Capra, Fritjof, 121
Catholicism, 80, 105
celestial archetype, sacred architecture reflecting, 88–89
chapter (*fasl*), 34
China, 98
Chinese Muslims, 206
Chinese tradition, mirror symbols in, 169
Chittick, William, 11, 53
Christ, 201
  bodily ascension of, 38
  Christianity centering, 45
  Ibn 'Arabi on, 46–47

Christian Mass, 198–199
Christianity, 38, 62, 80, 96, 176, 181–182
  Christ centered in, 45
  Islam contrasted with, 70–73, 83, 97, 113–114
  Islamic mysticism influenced by, 44
  medieval, 200
  physical archaeological evidence impacting, 201
  Sufism and, 46–47
  Western, 115–116
Christic Sufis, 46
city, Islamic traditional, 85–86
collective unconscious, 127, 129
colonization, British, 205
configuration (*shakl*), form confused with, 171
Confucianism, 206
contemplative states, sacred art externalizing, 171
Coomaraswamy, Ananda, 126, 133
  The Bugbear of Literacy by, 193
  on sacred art, 13
  symbols studied by, 124
Corbin, Henry, 12, 122–123, 127, 147
  L'homme de lumière dans le soufisme iranien by, 20
  L'imagination créatrice dans le soufisme d'Ibn 'Arabi by, 63
  "The Musical Sense of Persian Mysticism" by, 145–146
  Shi'ism attracting, 158
  Suhrawardi interpreted by, 20–23
  Temple et contemplation by, 89
Corodoba Mosque, 54
Corpus Hermeticum (treatises), 152
cosmic consciousness, 39–40
cosmology, 78
  angelology linked with, 57–58
  art compared with, 68–69
  Divine Principle pointed to by, 50
  Divine Reality reflected by, 5, 50, 53–54
  of Ibn 'Arabi, 61, 68–69
  illuminationist philosophy developing, 70
  the observer studying, 51
  across religions, 52
  spiritualization in relation to, 60
  Sufism and, 4–6
  of Suhrawardi, 69
  within tradition, 50
  traditional art compared with, 49
  See also Islamic cosmology; traditional cosmology
cosmos, and theophany, 74
creative power, imagination as, 144
creativity
  in modernity, 25
  religions inspiring, 32
  Sufism and, 2–4, 29
  See also art; imagination
Critchlow, Keith, 109

dancing, 38–39
Dante (poet), 30, 32, 142, 199
Davies, Paul, 120
Defoe, Daniel, 70–73
democracy, 203
The Demon Haunted World (Sagan), 197
Dickens, Charles, 115
al-din al-hanif. *See* primordial monotheism
al-Din 'Iraqi, Fakhr, 159
al-Din Kubra, Najm, 68
the Divine, art evoking, 14–15
Divine Comedy (Dante), 30, 32, 142, 199
Divine Principle, 3, 94, 151
  cosmology pointing to, 50
  religions embracing, 102
  science of, 52
  Supreme, 102
Divine Reality, 28, 37, 40, 62, 93, 101, 122
  cosmologies reflecting, 5, 50, 53–54
  imaginal world manifesting in, 64
  Sufi practices reaching, 40–41
  Sufism exploring, 35
  Sufism leading to, 5, 19
  symbols rooted in, 128
Diwan of Shams-i Tabrizi (Rumi), 146, 156
doctrine of Unity (*tawhid*), 21
dualism (*thuna'iyyah*), 79
  Cartesian, 76, 81, 121
  modern science founded on, 194
  quantum mechanics and, 81
  Suhrawardi against, 22

the East, the West contrasted with, 79–80
Eastern sciences, environment safeguarded by, 107–108
economic development, dangerousness of, 104
Egypt, 189
Eliade, Mircea, 95, 98–99, 124–125
Eliot, T. S., 31
the elite (*al-khawass*), 202–204
emptiness, 172, 185–186
Enlightenment, European, 195
environment, 1
  destruction of, 104
  Eastern sciences safeguarding, 107–108
  Islamic urban design integrating, 118
  Muslims mistreating, 116
  Sufism and, 8–9
  See also nature
environmental crisis, 6, 16, 193
  Industrial Revolution causing, 114–115
  metaphysics and, 7
  modern science and, 196–197
  as spiritual crisis, 109–110
  technology impacting, 103
equilibrium, nature reestablishing, 112
erotic mystical poetry, by Hafiz, 135–136
esoterism, theology and, 202
essence, archetypes contrasted with, 170
Essence of the Divine (*hahut*), 61

eternity, Sufi poetry
    witnessing, 136
ethics, order of nature in
    relation to, 99–100
Europe, poetry in, 141–142
European Enlightenment, 195
exile, of spiritual persons,
    35–36
expansion (*inshirah*), 186

fall of man, nature and,
    109–112
fana'. See annihilation
fasl. See chapter
fasting from talking (*sawm
    al-kalam*), 154–155
Firdawsi (poet), 184
fitrah, 5, 83
    Islam emphasizing, 75,
        84–85
    memory and, 75, 82
    nature returned to through,
        98
    poetry activating, 10–11
    Sufism reaching, 59
form (*surah*)
    configuration confused
        with, 171
    inner meaning juxtaposed
        with, 170
    meaning contrasted with, 25
forty (*arba'in*), 132
free verse (*al-shi'r al-hurr*), 26
Freudianism, 128
*Fundamental Symbols of Sacred
    Science* (Guénon), 125
Fusus al-hikam. See *Bezels of
    Wisdom*
al-Futuhat al-Makkiyyah (Ibn
    Arabi), 69, 174

Gaia hypothesis, 101
the general public (*al-'awam*),
    203
geometry, 177–178, 184
ghaflah. See negligence
gharib. See stranger
God, 53
    beauty authored by, 167–168
    Names and Qualities of,
        41–42, 62
    spiritual persons plucked
        by, 166–167
    Sufi Names for, 161
    as supreme artist, 180–181
    Unity of, 153
Grand Diwan (Rumi), 26
Greater Mysteries, 51
Guénon, René, 124–125, 193

habib. See beloved
Hadith, 11, 20–21, 35, 58, 60, 134
hadraat, 61, 67
Hafiz (poet), 135–136, 159
hahut. See Essence of the
    Divine
hajj, symbolism of, 89
haqiqah. See truth
al-haqiqah al-Muhammadiyyah.
    See Muhammadan Reality
al-haqq (attributes of God), 44
harmonics
    Islamic architecture of, 184
    within Ka'bah, 89–90
    proportions in, 148–149
harmony
    between humanity and
        nature, 8
    rituals reestablishing, 8,
        93–95
    within violence, 112

Hayy Ibn Yaqzan (Ibn Tufayl), 70–73
he (*huwa*), 161
Heaven, rituals from, 89
hedonism, 207
Hegel, 95, 96
Heidegger, Martin
  Being and Time by, 122
  Mulla Sadra differentiated from, 123
  technology critiqued by, 121–122
Heisenberg, Werner, 78
Heraclitus, 169
heretic (*mushrik*), 44
Hermes (god), 152
higher criticism, 200–201
hikmah adamiyyah. See Adamic wisdom
hikmah musawiyyah. See Mosaic wisdom
Hinduism, 10, 98, 121, 202
  Campbell believing in, 126–127
  Islam working with, 204–206
  Sufism encountering, 153
history, nature and, 95–98
History of Religions (Eliade), 98
hiya. See she
homes, traditional, 85–86
L'homme de lumière dans le soufisme iranien (Corbin), 20
human being, nature and, 93–94
human order (*nasut*), 169
human soul, pollution of, 6–7
humanity, nature between humanity and, 8
humans, the universe in relation to, 90
huwa. See he

I (*ana*), 161–162
the I (*inni*), the One separated from, 161
Ibn 'Arabi, M., 53, 63, 159, 162–163, 204, 206
  Bezels of Wisdom by, 46
  on Christ, 46–47
  cosmology of, 61, 68–69
  on metaphysics, 61
Ibn al-Farid, 10, 133, 139–140, 149
Ibn Malik, 138
Ibn Sina, 63–64, 119, 144, 149
Ibn Tufayl, 70–73
Ibn Tulun Mosque, 54
idolatry, Semites threatened by, 181
Idris (prophet), 152
Ilahi-Namah ('Attar), 162
illuminationist philosophy (*ishraqi* philosophy), 61, 70, 181, 183–184
imaginal, imaginary distinguished from, 63–64
imaginal world (*'alam al-khayal*), 63, 69–70
  art in relation to, 65
  Divine Reality manifesting, 64
  physical world surrounded by, 66

imaginary, imaginal
    distinguished from, 63–64
imagination
    as creative power, 144
    Islamic cosmology and, 63
    philosophers on, 63
    spirituality without, 65
*L'imagination créatrice dans
    le soufisme d'Ibn 'Arabi*
    (Corbin), 63
immanence (*tashbih*),
    transcendence in relation
    to, 191
The Implicate Order (Bohm), 78
inclusiveness, Sufism
    characterized by, 2–3
India, 187, 205
Industrial Revolution,
    environmental crisis
    caused by, 114–115
I-ness (*ana'iyyah*), 161
initiatic pact (*bay'ah*), 37
inner meaning, form
    juxtaposed with, 170
inner silence, sacred art
    externalizing, 172
inni. *See* the I
innovation (*bid'ah*), 37
inshirah. *See* expansion
intellect (*'aql*), 66, 71–72, 154, 177
*An Introduction to Islamic
    Cosmological Doctrines*
    (Nasr), 3, 49, 55, 57
ishraqi philosophy. *See*
    illuminationist philosophy
Islam, 55
    balance emphasized in,
        207–208
    Buddhism compared with,
        186
    Christianity contrasted with,
        70–73, 83, 97, 113–114
    fitrah emphasized in, 75,
        84–85
    without higher criticism, 201
    Hinduism working with,
        204–206
    mysticism in, 36, 44
    nature dealt with in, 116
    phenomenology not fitting,
        99
    religions synthesized in,
        45–46, 56
    remembrance centered in,
        82–84
    space sacralized in, 88
    symbols in, 192
    See also Muslims; Qur'an;
        Sufism
*Islam and the Plight of Modern
    Man* (Nasr), 105
El-Islam Christianizado
    (Palacios), 47
Islamic architecture, 176
    destruction of, 16
    Gothic contrasted with, 87
    of harmonics, 184
    Islamic cosmology in
        relation to, 186–189
    Ka'bah centered in, 184–185
    nature maximized in, 117
Islamic art, 54, 150–151
    mathematics centered in,
        177–178
    Persian contrasted with
        Arab, 181–182

Islamic art *(continued)*
  Pythagoras influencing, 175
  sculpture excluded in, 182–183
Islamic Art and Spirituality (Nasr), 147
Islamic civilization, poetry centered in, 133–134, 138–139
Islamic cosmology, 3, 49, 55, 57
  imagination and, 63
  Islamic architecture in relation to, 186–189
  symbols within, 67–68
Islamic gnosis (*ma'rifah*), 2, 20–21
Islamic mysticism, Christianity influencing, 44
Islamic philosophers, 28, 63
Islamic traditional city, the sacred flowing within, 85–86
Islamic urban design, environment integrated into, 118
Izutsu, Toshihiko, 186

jabarut. See angelic world; archangelic world
Jami, 'Abd al-Rahman, 162
jinn (psychic beings), 66–67
Judaism, 176
Jung, C., 123, 126, 127–128, 129
Jungianism, tradition subverted by, 128

Ka'bah (building), 88
  harmonics within, 89–90
  Islamic architecture centering, 184–185
  stability represented by, 208
Kant, Emanuel, 120
Kepler (mathematician), 12, 148–149
al-khawass. See elite
al-Khayyam, Omar, 107, 143
al-Khidr (prophet), 157–158
knowledge (*shu'ur*), 144–145
  beauty and, 13
  divine, 20, 24, 155, 157
  poetry in relation to, 30
  pure, 196
Knowledge and the Sacred (Nasr), 72
Koyré, Alexandre, 194
Küng, Hans, 199, 202

lahut. See Names and Qualities of God
Lame Deer, John, 8
language, intellect impregnating, 154
Lesser Mysteries, 51
letters, Arabic, 174
Lewisohn, Leonard, 2, 14
Light, Suhrawardi centering, 23
the Light of lights (*nur al-anwar*), 23
Lings, Martin, 89–90
lute (*'ud*), 167

macrocosm (*al-'alam-al-kabir*), 39

Madinah (city), 85
Maharshi, Sri Ramana, 128
Man and Nature (Nasr), 6–7, 14, 102, 118
ma'na. See meaning
ma'rifah. See Islamic gnosis
Marxism, 203
Masirati ila'l-Haqq. See *My Journey to the Truth*
Mass, Christian, 198–199
mathematics, 175, 204
  Islamic art centering, 177–178
  metaphysics in relation to, 14
  music and, 149–150
  See also Pythagoras
Mathnawi (Rumi), 134
Mawaqif. See *Stations*
Mazdaism, 183
McClain, Ernest, 89–90
meaning (*ma'na*), form contrasted with, 25, 170
memory, 82–84
metaphors, symbols contrasted with, 136
metaphysics, 71–72, 100, 168, 206
  environmental crisis and, 7
  higher criticism inverting, 200
  Ibn 'Arabi on, 61
  mathematics in relation to, 14
  science in relation to, 118–120
  symbols for, 178
Meyer, Hans, 199

microcosm (*al-'alam al-saghir*), 39
miniatures, 182–183
mi'raj. See ascension
al-mi'raj. See nocturnal ascension
al-mi'raj al-jismani. See bodily accession
mirror symbols, 170
  in Chinese tradition, 169
  in Sufism, 168
  traditionalists evoking, 13
al-mizan. See balance
modern science
  dualism founding, 194
  environmental crisis and, 196–197
  religions in relation to, 15
  See also quantum mechanics; technology
modernity
  The Bugbear of Literacy criticizing, 193
  creativity in, 25
  poetry influenced by, 29–30
  prayers in, 16–17, 197–198
  sacred science lost to, 197
  Sufism and, 2, 15–17
  tradition broken from in, 26
monotheist (*muwahhid*), 151–153
Mosaic wisdom (*hikmah musawiyyah*), 46
mosques, 54, 117
  emptiness characterizing, 185
  traditional architecture lacked in, 188–189

mosques *(continued)*
  virgin nature re-created in, 85
  See also *Ka'bah*
Muhammad (prophet), as "Seal of Prophets," 56
Muhammadan grace (*al-barakah al-muhammadiyyah*), 19–20
Muhammadan Reality (*al-haqiqah al-Muhammadiyah*), 41
mulk. See physical world
mushrik. See heretic
music, 145–146
  Divine contrasted with human, 147
  mathematics and, 149–150
  poetry and silence and, 12, 155
  silent, 12, 147–148
  Sufi poetry intertwined with, 146
  See also harmonics
"The Musical Sense of Persian Mysticism" (Corbin), 145–146
Muslim daily prayers (*salat*), 198–199
Muslim thinkers, Pythagoras inspiring, 151–152
Muslims
  Chinese, 206
  environment mistreated by, 116
  Madinah lived in by, 85
muwahhid. See monotheist
My Journey to the Truth (Masirati ila'l-Haqq) (al-Yashrutiyyah), 163

mysticism
  in Islam, 36, 44
  Platonism and Neoplatonism provided by, 24
  surrealism inspired by, 29
  See also Sufism
The Myth of the Eternal Return (Eliade), 95
myths, 123–125

Names and Qualities of God (*lahut*), 41–42, 62
Naqshbandi Order, 156
Nasr, Seyyed Hossein, 3
nasut. See human order
Native Americans, 95, 101, 190
naturalism, miniatures avoiding, 183
nature, 7, 78
  degradation of, 104
  equilibrium reestablished by, 112
  fall of man and, 109–112
  fitrah returning to, 98
  harmony between humanity and, 8
  history and, 95–98
  human being and, 93–94
  Islam dealing with, 116
  Islamic architecture maximizing, 117
  in Qur'an, 88
  religions in relation to, 118
  science of, 79–80
  technology controlling, 110
  temple in relation to, 84
  virgin, 84–85

Nazm al-suluk (Ibn al-Farid), 133
The Need for a Sacred Science (Nasr), 3, 9, 105, 199
negligence (*ghaflah*), 37, 75
Neoplatonism, 23–25
New Age movement, 40, 105–106, 197
new physics, traditional cosmology separated from, 80–81
New Testament, 141
Niffari, A., 25, 26
nocturnal ascension (*al-mi'raj*), 38
nun (letter), 174–175
nur al-anwar. *See* the Light of lights

observation of the stars (*rasd*), 43
the observer, cosmology studied by, 51
the One, I separated from, 161
Oneness (*tawhid*), 56
order of nature, ethics in relation to, 99–100

Pakistan, 205
Palacios, Asín, 47
Parmenides, 169
perennial philosophy, 28
Perfect Man, 41–42
Persia, 20, 23
Persians, Arabs contrasted with, 181–182
pessimism, 102–103
Peter (saint), 201
phenomenology, Islam not fitting into, 99

philosophers
 on imagination, 63
 Islamic, 28, 63
 physicists and, 120
 See also specific philosophers
philosophy, perennial, 28
physical world (*mulk*), 62, 66
physicists, philosophers and, 120
physics, 119
Plato, 91, 148
 reading, 21
 on recollection, 82–83
 Schuon and Nasr emphasizing, 168
Platonism, 24–25, 175–176
Plotinus, 152, 168
Poems of the Way (Nasr), 9, 131, 155, 160
poetical languages, Sufism integrating, 25
poetry (*shi'r*), 30–31
 in Europe, 141–142
 fitrah activated by, 10–11
 Islamic civilization centering, 133–134, 138–139
 knowledge in relation to, 30
 modernity influencing, 29–30
 music and silence and, 12, 155
 popularity of, 32–33
 religious performances and, 10–11
 silence written by, 137–138
 Sufism and, 9–13, 33–34
 symbols expressed in, 155, 190

poetry *(continued)*
  tradition and, 29
  the West casting aside, 142–144
  See also Sufi poetry
poets (*al-shu'ara'*), 134
pollution, of human soul, 6–7
Pound, Ezra, 31
praxis, the sacred accessed through, 127
prayers, 87, 89
  canonical, 86
  in modernity, 16–17, 197–198
  Muslim daily, 198–199
Présence de Louis Massignon (Nasr), 44
primordial monotheism (*al-din al-hanif*), 28
prostration (*sujud*), 86
psyche (*nafs*), 161
psychological world, 82, 128
pure knowledge, science contrasted with, 196
Pythagoras, 148–149
  Egyptian and ancient Persian teachings influencing, 176–177
  Islamic art influenced by, 175
  Muslim thinkers inspired by, 151–152
  Sufism influenced by, 150–151
Pythagoreanism, Abrahamic, 150–151, 175–176

qira'ah. See readings
Qissat al-ghurbat al-gharbiyyah. See The Tale of the Occidental Exile

The Quantum Enigma (Smith, W.), 78
quantum mechanics, 77–78
  Boehr interpreting, 76
  dualism and, 81
  traditional cosmology studying, 79
al-Qummi, Qadi Sa'id, 89
Qur'an, 97, 141, 201
  Abraham and Jesus included in, 21
  brittleness of this world emphasized in, 207–208
  calligraphy illustrating, 172–173
  nature in, 88
  Sufi poetry citing, 133–134
Qur'anic medieval exegesis (*ta'wil*), 199–200
Qur'anic recitation (*tajwid*), 172–173

Raine, Kathleen, 145
Ramadan (month of fasting, Muslim calender), 154
Ramayana (sacred book), 10
rasd. See observation of the stars
readings (*qira'ah*), 173
Reality, Divine. *See* Divine Reality
reality, traditional art powered by, 190
recollection, Plato on, 82–83
Religion and the Order of Nature (Nasr), 6, 93, 102, 118
religions
  cosmology across, 52

creativity inspired by, 32
Divine Principle embraced
   by, 102
Islam synthesizing, 45–46,
   56
modern science in relation
   to, 15
nature in relation to, 118
Schuon on unity of, 102
science of, 99
unity of, 102, 133
the West lacking, 106
See also Christianity;
   Hinduism; Islam
religious performances, poetry
   and, 10–11
remembrance, Islam centering,
   82–84
the Renaissance, 194
Risalat al-'ishq (Ibn Sina), 149
rituals, 8–9
   harmony reestablished
      through, 8, 93–95
   from Heaven, 89
   of Sufi orders, 37
Robinson Crusoe (Defoe), 70–73
romanticism, 143
Ruba'iyyat (al-Khayyam), 107
Rumi, Jalal al-Din, 1, 10–11,
   107, 137, 140, 204
   Diwan of Shams-i Tabrizi by,
      146, 156
   Grand Diwan by, 26
   Mathnawi by, 134
   on traditional art, 166

the sacred
   within Islamic traditional
      city, 85–86

   praxis accessing, 127
   science divorced from, 123
   the secular not
      distinguished from,
      204–206
   symbols lit by, 124–125
sacred architecture, celestial
   archetype reflected by,
   88–89
sacred art
   arithmetic as basis for, 177
   contemplative states
      externalized through, 171
   Coomaraswamy on, 13
   inner silence externalized
      by, 172
   Qur'anic recitation as, 173
sacred dancing, 38–39
sacred geography, 69–70
sacred geometry, 177–178
sacred science, 9, 15–16, 108–
   109, 197
Sadra, Mulla, 64, 122–123
al-Safa', Ikhwan, 177
Sagan, Carl, 197
salat. *See* canonical prayer;
   Muslim daily prayers
Sanskrit, 141
De Santillana, Giorgio, 194
sawm al-kalam. *See* fasting
   from talking
Schimmel, Annemarie, 11,
   134
Schuon, Frithjof, 44, 96, 151,
   187–188, 193
   To Have a Center by, 199
   Plato emphasized by Nasr
      and, 168
   on unity of religions, 102

science, 125
  of Divine Principle, 52
  metaphysics in relation to, 118–120
  of nature, 79–80
  pure knowledge contrasted with, 196
  of religions, 99
  sacred, 9, 15–16, 108–109, 197
  the sacred divorced from, 123
  the West emphasizing, 195
  See also modern science
Scientific Revolution, 80, 194
sculpture, Islam art excluding, 182–183
The Secret Garden of Divine Mysteries (Shabistari), 139
The Secrets of Worship (*Asrar al-'ibadat*) (al-Qummi), 89
the secular, the sacred not distinguished from, 204–206
seeing, being contrasted with, 14
The Self-Disclosure of God (Chittick), 53
Semites, idolatry threatening, 181
Shabistari, Mahmud, 10, 139
Shadhiliyyah Order, 36
Shah-namah (Firdawsi), 184
shakl. *See* configuration
Shari'ah, 163
she (*hiya*), 161
al-Shifa' (Ibn Sina), 149
Shi'ism, 157–158
Shintoism, 187

shi'r. *See* poetry
al-shi'r al-hurr. *See* free verse
al-shu'ara'. *See* poets
shu'ur. *See* knowledge
silence
  inner, 172
  music and poetry and, 12, 155
  poetry writing, 137–138
  words creating, 140–141, 145–146, 153–155
silent music, 12, 147–148
Silent Music (Nasr), 147–148
Smith, Huston, 14, 119
Smith, Wolfgang, 78, 81, 109
sonoral art, 14
sophia perennis, Sufism within, 2–3
the soul, Sufism training, 156
space, Islam sacralizing, 88
spiritual crisis, environmental crisis as, 109–110
spiritual lineage, Sufism transmitting, 157
spiritual path (*tariqah*), 29, 41
spiritual persons
  exile of, 35–36
  God plucking, 166–167
  symbols seen by, 191
spirituality, 15, 65
spiritualization, cosmology in relation to, 60
stability, Ka'bah representing, 208
Stations (*Mawaqif*) (Niffari), 25, 26
Steuco, Augustino, 28
stranger (*gharib*), 35
Sufi Essays (Nasr), 7, 35

Sufi masters, 156–160
Sufi Names, for God, 161
Sufi orders (*tariqah*), 36–37, 159, 160
Sufi poetry, 139
  eternity witnessed in, 136
  music intertwined with, 146
  Qur'an cited in, 133–134
  Sufi masters of, 156–159
Sufi practices, Divine Reality reached for through, 40–41
Sufis (California group), 105–106
Sufis, Christic, 46
Sufism
  art and, 13, 165–166
  Christianity and, 46–47
  cosmology and, 4–6
  creativity and, 2–4, 29
  Divine Reality explored by, 35
  Divine Reality led to through, 5, 19
  environment and, 6–9
  fitrah reached for, 59
  Hinduism encountered by, 153
  inclusiveness characterizing, 2–3
  Islamic gnosis characterized by, 2
  mirror symbols in, 168
  modernity decried in, 2, 15–17
  poetical languages integrated into, 25
  poetry and, 9–13, 33–34
  Pythagoras influencing, 150–151
  within sophia perennis, 2–3
  the soul trained through, 156
  spiritual femininity of, 163–164
  spiritual lineage transmitting, 157
  Universal Man normalized within, 42
  women in, 162–164
Suhrawardi, 43
  Corbin interpreting, 20–23
  cosmology of, 69
  against dualism, 22
  Light centered by, 23
  The Tale of the Occidental Exile by, 36
sujud. See prostration
Sultan Ahmad Mosque, 54
Sultan Hasan Mosque, 117
Sun Dance, 95
Sung dynasty, 186
supreme artist, God as, 180–181
Supreme Divine Principle, 102
surah. See form
surrealism, mysticism inspiring, 29
symbolism, of *hajj*, 89
symbolized, symbols unifying with, 15
symbols, 184
  Coomaraswamy studying, 124
  Divine Reality as root of, 128
  in Islam, 192
  within Islamic cosmology, 67–68

symbols *(continued)*
  metaphors contrasted with, 136
  for metaphysics, 178
  poetry expressing, 155, 190
  power of, 190
  the sacred lighting, 124–125
  spiritual persons seeing, 191
  symbolized unifying with, 15
  across traditions, 123
  See also mirror symbols

Tabrizi, Shams-i, 159
tajalli. See theophany
tajwid. See Qur'anic recitation
The Tale of the Occidental Exile (*Qissat al-ghurbat al-gharbiyyah*) (Suhrawardi), 36
tanzih. See transcendence
The Tao of Physics (Capra), 77, 121
Taoism, 98, 121, 186
tariqah. See spiritual path; Sufi order
tashbih. See immanence
tawhid. See doctrine of Unity; Oneness; unity; Unity of God
ta'wil. See Qur'anic medieval exegesis
technology, 104–105
  environmental crisis impacted by, 103
  Heidegger critiquing, 121–122
  nature controlled by, 110

temple, nature in relation to, 84
Temple et contemplation (Corbin), 89
theological modernism, Qur'anic medieval exegesis differentiated from, 199–200
theology
  Christian, 62, 71, 73
  esoterism and, 202
  Western Christianity overrationalizing, 115–116
theophany (*tajalli*), 44, 74, 169
thuna'iyyah. See dualism
To Have a Center (Schuon), 199
Toynbee, Arnold, 195
tradition
  anti-, 27
  Chinese, 169
  cosmology within, 50
  different human types catered to by, 55
  Jungianism subverting, 128
  modernity breaking from, 26
  poetry and, 29
traditional architecture, mosques lacking, 188–189
traditional art
  cosmology compared with, 49
  reality powering, 190
  Rumi on, 166
traditional city, Islamic, 85–86
traditional cosmology
  new physics separated from, 80–81

psychological world accounted for in, 82
quantum mechanics studied by, 79
traditional homes, 85–86
traditionalists, mirror symbols evoked by, 13
traditions, symbols across, 123
transcendence (*tanzih*), immanence in relation to, 191
truth (*haqiqah*), 161
Twelfth Imam, 158

"'U" (Persian pronoun), 161
'*ud*. *See* lute
ugliness, art and, 179–180
Ultimate Reality. *See* Divine Reality
unity (*tawhid*), 102, 133, 177
Unity of Being (*wahdat al-wujud*), 3–4, 61
Unity of God (*tawhid*), 153
Unity of Reality (*wahdat al-wujud*), 41–44
Universal Man, 41–43
the universe, humans in relation to, 90
urban civilization, 116–117
urban design, Islamic, 118
al-Urjuzah fi'l-tibb (Ibn Sina), 138

Valmiki (poet), 10
violence, harmony within, 112
virgin nature, 84–85
voyage, 58–59, 72

wahdat al-wujud. *See* Unity of Being; Unity of Reality
Walad, Baha' al-Din, 159
wayfaring, 59, 61
the West, 113–115
 as anti-traditional civilization, 27
 atheists produced in, 202
 the East contrasted with, 79–80
 poetry cast aside in, 142–144
 religions lacked in, 106
 science emphasized in, 195
Western Christianity, theology overrationalized by, 115–116
Western poets, Arab and Persian poets emulating, 30–31, 137
wind catchers, 117
Wolf-Gazo, Ernest, 3
women, in Sufism, 162–164
words
 art of expressing, 173
 al-'Attar on, 153
 silence created from, 140–141, 145–146, 153–155
al-wujud. *See* being

al-Yashrutiyyah, Fatimah, 163
al-Yashrutiyyah Order, 163
Yeats, William Butler, 31, 124

zawiyah, 30, 36
Zimmer, Heinrich, 126
Zoroastrianism, 20, 22, 187